SAT ELA in the Classroom

Bring SAT ELA prep into the classroom to enhance student learning! In this new copublication from Routledge and test-prep experts A-List Education, you'll learn how the updated SAT exam is closely aligned with the Common Core, making it easy to weave test prep into your curriculum and help students hone the skills they need for college readiness. The book is filled with practical examples of how the Common Core State Standards are connected to specific sections, question types, and strategies applicable to the SAT, so you can simultaneously prepare your students for the test while improving their reading, writing, and language skills.

   Bonus: A Study Guide to help you use the book for school-wide professional development is available as a free eResource download from our website: www.routledge.com/9781138668300.

A-List Education is an educational services provider serving more than 50,000 students with tutoring programs across the U.S. as well as in the UK, Dubai, Switzerland, and China.

Other Books Available From Routledge and A-List Education
(www.routledge.com/eyeoneducation)

SAT Math in the Classroom:
Integrating Assessments, Standards, and Instruction

ACT ELA in the Classroom:
Integrating Assessments, Standards, and Instruction

ACT Math in the Classroom:
Integrating Assessments, Standards, and Instruction

SAT ELA in the Classroom

Integrating Assessments, Standards, and Instruction

A-List Education

First published 2017
by Routledge
711 Third Avenue, New York, NY 10017

and by Routledge
2 Park Square, Milton Park, Abingdon, Oxon, OX14 4RN

*Routledge is an imprint of the Taylor & Francis Group,
an informa business*

© 2017 Taylor & Francis

The right of A-List Education to be identified as author of this work has been asserted by them in accordance with sections 77 and 78 of the Copyright, Designs and Patents Act 1988.

All rights reserved. No part of this book may be reprinted or reproduced or utilised in any form or by any electronic, mechanical, or other means, now known or hereafter invented, including photocopying and recording, or in any information storage or retrieval system, without permission in writing from the publishers.

Trademark notice: Product or corporate names may be trademarks or registered trademarks, and are used only for identification and explanation without intent to infringe.

Library of Congress Cataloging-in-Publication Data
Names: A-List Education, author.
Title: SAT ELA in the classroom : integrating assessments, standards, and
    instruction / by A-List Education.
Description: New York, NY : Routledge, 2017.
Identifiers: LCCN 2016009871 | ISBN 9781138668294 (hardback) |
    ISBN 9781138668300 (pbk.) | ISBN 9781315618708 (e-book)
Subjects: LCSH: English language—Study and teaching (Secondary)—
    United States. | Common Core State Standards (Education) | SAT
    (Educational test)
Classification: LCC LB1631 .A25 2017 | DDC 428.0071/2—dc23
LC record available at https://lccn.loc.gov/2016009871

ISBN: 978-1-138-66829-4 (hbk)
ISBN: 978-1-138-66830-0 (pbk)
ISBN: 978-1-315-61870-8 (ebk)

Typeset in Palatino
by Apex CoVantage, LLC

Printed and bound in the United States of America by Sheridan

Contents

eResources vii
About the Author ix
Introduction and Overview xi

1 About the SAT 1
  Format 3
  Reading 5
  Writing and Language 10
  Essay 12
  Changes to the Test 15

2 Alignment With Common Core ELA Standards 19
  How to Read the ELA Standards 19
  Alignment 20
  How to Read This Section 22
  Alignment Beyond the Test 25
  Reading 26
  Writing 46
  Language 63
  Other Topics 79

3 Reading Assignments 81
  Choosing a Passage 82
  Writing the Questions 86
  Giving the Assignment 95
  Sample Passage 98
  Sample Questions 100
  Answers and Explanations 101

4 Writing Assignments 105
  Format 106
  Practice Tests 108
  Revision 111
  Expand the Assignment 114
  Essay Assignment Summary 117

  Appendix: All ELA Alignment Tables 119
  Additional Resources 133

eResources

This book is accompanied by free online eResources, including a Study Guide to help you work on this book with colleagues, as well as additional materials to help you with school-wide implementation of the ideas in this book. To access the eResources, go to www.routledge.com/9781138668300 and click on the eResources tab. Then click on the items you'd like to view. They will begin downloading to your computer.

About the Author

A-List Education was founded in 2005 with a mission to bring innovation and opportunity to education, empowering students to reach their true potential. We work with schools, school districts, families, and nonprofits and provide tailored solutions for specific learning and curriculum needs—ultimately working to improve college readiness and access. Our staff comprises experienced and passionate educators each with a distinctive and personal approach to academic success, and our management team collectively possesses more than 75 years of tutoring, teaching, and test preparation experience. We now provide leading-edge education services and products to more than 500 high schools and nonprofit organizations, helping more than 70,000 students a year in the United States and around the world.

A-List has a variety of offerings for SAT and ACT preparation, including:

- **Textbooks** for students studying individually or for teachers conducting classes. Our content not only emphasizes test-taking techniques but also reinforces core skills, which empower students for academic success long after taking the test.
- **Professional development** to help schools and organizations set up their own courses. Our seminars create valuable educational expertise that will allow teachers in your district to bring content and problem-solving strategies directly into their classrooms.
- **Direct course instruction** using our own staff. Our dedicated and experienced teachers receive intensive training before entering the classroom and have proven track records of empowering students to reach their academic potential.
- An **online portal** to remotely grade practice tests and provide supplemental material. This platform removes the burden of grading complex tests without requiring customized technology and provides supplemental material for your ongoing courses.

x ◆ About the Author

◆ Individual one-on-one **tutoring**. Our instructors help students deliver average improvements of more than three times the national average in the United States. In addition, our students routinely gain acceptance to their top choice schools and have been awarded millions of dollars in scholarships.

Visit us at **www.alisteducation.com** to learn more.

Introduction and Overview

The SAT and the Common Core

The Common Core State Standards Initiative (CCSSI) is a program designed to unify the state standards across the United States so that students, parents, and educators have a clear sense of what skills students must acquire in school to become ready for college or a career. It is an independent initiative in which states may voluntarily choose to participate, but by the end of 2015, 42 states plus the District of Columbia had chosen to adopt the standards. The standards are designed to be rigorous, clear, and consistent, and they are based on real evidence to align with the knowledge and skill necessary for life beyond high school.

The program is controversial to be sure, but a strong foundation is already in place, and schools around the country are working to align their own materials and programs with the newly adopted standards. The standards specifically do not outline exact requirements for curriculum, such that schools and districts can still make their own choices about how to run their classes while still adhering to the standards. As a result, some schools may struggle to find the right material.

However, there already exists a comprehensive source of material that addresses the wide range of skills and knowledge that the Common Core emphasizes: the SAT.

Not all schools currently offer preparation programs for the SAT, but even those that do tend to treat the test as distinct from normal schoolwork. The test is seen as supplementary, and preparation is an unpleasant game in which students learn tricks to game the system without actually learning skills. This view of the test, however, is not just uncharitable but false. In fact, SAT preparation can fill many of the gaps to help schools align their curricula with the Common Core.

The SAT requires students to use many of the same math and reading skills that are the goals of the standards. It is designed to identify whether students are ready for college by testing them on the skills and knowledge they will need when they get there. In fact, the designer of the SAT, the College Board, was actively involved in the creation of the standards, and their own research about college readiness was integral to the program. Furthermore, recent changes to the test in 2016 were initiated in no small part to bring the test further in alignment with the standards.

Preparing for the test can accomplish two goals at once. Test preparation's primary goal is to prepare for the test itself, helping students maximize their scores on the test and thus improving their chances of being admitted to the colleges of their choice. Beyond pure admissions, students' test scores can have a number of uses for different programs and institutions. For example,

- **College admissions**. Roughly half of a student's admissions profile is composed of a combination of GPA and SAT or ACT score. A high score can be a huge differentiator for the majority of elite universities and a minimum hurdle for the majority of state universities.
- **Scholarships**. There are billions of dollars of aid in private and school-based scholarship money tied directly to test scores.
- **Community colleges**. Even at community colleges with low graduation rates, good scores can allow students to avoid placement in remedial classes.
- **Military**. For students interested in the military, baseline scores can qualify a student for officer training as opposed to regular enlistment.
- **State assessment**. The SAT is increasingly used as a statewide student assessment to identify achievement of particular benchmarks.

But test preparation is also a valuable activity in itself; students will also be working on honing and strengthening the skills they need for college readiness. Furthermore, the test material itself is valuable even beyond their application to the actual test. The passages, essay prompts, and mathematical concepts contained herein can be divorced from the SAT. You do not have to actually take the SAT to draw value from reading and analyzing its passages, analyzing its grammatical structures, or attempting its math problems.

It is for these reasons that some states have decided to use the SAT as its primary measurement for high school achievement, rather than a more explicitly standards-based assessment.

Alignment

In 2010, the College Board produced an alignment study to show how the standards align with the skills that the SAT assessed. The results of these studies show that the test significantly aligned with the standards.[1]

Since then, the test was radically changed starting with the PSAT in 2015 and the SAT in 2016. While the changes to the test were clearly motivated by alignment to the standards, the College Board has not yet produced an official alignment study for the new SAT. They have not officially said much to date about the Common Core specifically. In a guide to implementing the new test, in response to alignment with the CCSS, the document states: "The redesigned SAT measures the skills and knowledge that evidence shows are essential for college and career success. It is not aligned to any single set of standards." This seems to distance the test from the notion that the Common Core was the motivation for the redesign. But it also notes that the skills for the new SAT draw from the same evidence base as "state academic standards including the Common Core, the Texas Essential Knowledge and Skills, and the Virginia Standards for Learning—as well as in the best college-prep curricula."[2]

However, we at A-List want to take a closer look at how exactly the new test aligns with the Common Core. We have compared the old alignment document and the new test material to project the alignment for the new test.

What does this alignment tell us? Several things:

1. The redesigned test aligns strongly with the CCSS.
2. The redesigned test does not align *perfectly* with the CCSS. There are a number of standards that are not relevant to the SAT.
3. While some changes to the SAT have made it more aligned with the CCSS, others have made it less so. As a whole, the test isn't necessarily more aligned with the test than it already was.
4. *But the old SAT was already strongly aligned with the CCSS.*

The College Board's study demonstrated that the skills tested by the SAT align with the skills of the standards. This study is heavily researched and incredibly thorough. However, it has not been updated for the new test and it does not link these skills to real test material. This book will xiv ◆ Introduction and Overview

use that information to demonstrate specifically the connection between the test and the standards in a practical manner. Furthermore, this book will show that test material can be adapted and expanded to address even those standards that are outside the scope of the test.

About This Book

This book has two main goals:

1. To show how specific SAT ELA material aligns with the ELA CCSS.
2. To discuss how to incorporate SAT preparation into your regular ELA classes outside of an explicit test preparation class.

Why do we focus on the CCSS? First of all, because the grand majority of states use it. There's no shortage of debate about the value of the standards, but it's undeniable that they are in place throughout most of the country. Even some states that are moving away from the standards are doing so more in name than in practice and are keeping the content of the CCSS in place.

Of course, not every state uses CCSS, but it remains a useful framework for connecting SAT material to classroom material. We can't run through every state's particulars in one book, but the popularity of the CCSS make them a convenient reference. If you don't use them, you can still use CCSS as a touchstone to compare to your own state standards. Even if you do use CCSS, your state may also have its own assessments or graduation requirements that deviate from CCSS. The alignment information is one piece of the picture.

Second, some states are actually using the SAT as their main statewide assessment. They are generally doing so because of the SAT's alignment to the Common Core. Is this a good idea? That's debatable, and we won't take sides here. The question is part political, part pedagogical, often emotional. However, we can offer our research and expertise in the test so you can see for yourself where it coincides with your curriculum and where it doesn't.

Structure of the Book

Chapter 1 will describe the structure and content of the SAT's ELA sections for those who may be unfamiliar with the test, along with discussion of how the test has changed and some effective test-taking techniques. Keep in mind that this is a general overview. It draws information from our main textbook, *The Book of Knowledge*, which is the product of years of experience with the test and goes into much greater detail about the test's content and the most effective strategies.

Chapter 2 will connect the SAT to the Common Core ELA standards (Reading, Writing, and Language). This section will take a closer look to show where the test does and does not align with these standards. It will go through each individual standard one by one to discuss what specific sections, question types, or strategies align with the standard in question. Additional discussion also describes how, even when the test does not align with the standard, test material can be pushed beyond its intended scope in order to do so.

Chapters 3 and 4 will focus on how to use all this material in the classroom. This could mean using your classes as explicit preparation for the test; it could mean using test material to supplement your regular classes; it could mean preparing for the test as a tool with which to get your students to meet the standards; or it could be a combination of these things. This section will include some discussions and samples to help get you started.

The Appendix will list all of the alignment tables discussed in Chapter 2, followed by a bibliography and suggestions for further reading.

Notes

1. Interestingly, this document is no longer available on the College Board's website, possibly to avoid confusion between the old test and the new test. It is still possible to find it online hosted elsewhere with a bit of searching.
2. *College Board Guide to Implementing the Redesigned SAT*, October 2014, https://collegereadiness.collegeboard.org/pdf/college-board-guide-implementing-redesigned-sat-installment-2.pdf

1

About the SAT

The SAT is a college admissions test, first and foremost. It was designed for that purpose and has been used as such since 1926. In the century since its creation, it has substantially changed a number of times, but its primary goal has remained the same: to provide a standardized metric for colleges to be able to judge students from disparate backgrounds.

With the redesign of the SAT in 2016, however, the College Board has been trying to shift the focus of the test more towards the K–12 market. Much of the rhetoric surrounding the redesign centered around "real-world skills" and "math that matters most", eliminating "irrelevant vocabulary".

Of course, this is not the first time the SAT has been redesigned—most recently in 2005 when analogies were removed and the Writing component and essay were added, or in 1994 when calculators were first permitted and non-multiple-choice grid-in questions were added. It seems like every redesign has been surrounded by rhetoric of focusing on real-world, important skills. With this redesign, the College Board has made an active effort to emphasize college readiness benchmarks to a greater degree than they did before. They are re-organizing their suite of tests, including versions the PSAT starting as early as eighth grade, and moving toward a longitudinal assessment of benchmarks throughout high school. They are moving past the market of individual students taking the test for college and marketing their tests directly to schools, to be used both for college admissions and for skills assessment.

Is this a good idea? Who knows? Very limited data is currently available so it's impossible to say yet whether the test does a good job at assessing these skills. We don't even know how well the new test serves for admissions. The old SAT, when combined with high school GPA, was a stronger predictor of college performance than was either of those metrics alone. We shall see how the new test shapes up when we see more data and that new-test smell starts to wear off.

In the meantime, it's here, so we must acknowledge it and deal with it. While we don't know much about how the scores will shape up, we do know quite a bit about what's on the test, enough that we can make a concerted effort to prepare students for it.

We want to help you incorporate SAT material into your classroom in order to prepare students, without running an explicit SAT prep course. To do so, the first and most important thing is simply to know what's on the test and what the test is like. The best way to do that is firsthand: *you should absolutely do some official practice tests yourself.* There are four full-length SATs and one PSAT available for free download on the College Board's website. Go do one and see what you think.

In the meantime, we're not going to go through our whole prep book (it is, however, for sale on our website!), but we do want to give you an overview of the structure and content of the test.

Format

The SAT is split into two subjects, **Evidence-Based Reading and Writing** and **Mathematics**. The test has four sections, two for each of the subjects, plus an optional fifth section for the **Essay**. The test lasts 3 hours, or 3 hours and 50 minutes if you choose to do the essay.

Besides the Essay, most sections have only multiple-choice questions, with one exception: each Math section will contain some questions for which students must produce their own responses. All multiple-choice questions will have four possible choices.

The two sections for Evidence-Based Reading and Writing (henceforth called EBRAW) will cover two different content areas: **Reading** and **Writing and Language**. The two Mathematics sections will cover mostly the same material, but on one section calculators are permitted and on the other they are not.

Table 1.1 SAT Format

Section	Portion	Number of Questions	Time	Description
Evidence-Based Reading and Writing	1. Reading Test	52 questions	65 min	5 passages, each with 10–11 questions on reading comprehension
	2. Writing & Language Test	44 questions	35 min	4 passages, each with 11 questions on grammar, usage, and style
	Total	**96 questions**	**100 min**	
Math	3. No Calculator	20 questions	25 min	15 multiple-choice questions 5 student-produced response questions (grid-ins)
	4. Calculator OK	38 questions	55 min	30 multiple-choice questions 8 student-produced response questions (grid-ins)
	Total	**58 questions**	**80 min**	
Essay	*5. Essay*	*1 essay*	*50 min*	*Optional. One 1–4 page essay.*
	Total	**154 questions**	**3 hours**	
	with essay	*154 questions + 1 essay*	*3 hours 50 min*	

Scores

Each student will get a *Section Score* ranging from 200 to 800 for each of the two subjects. These scores are added together to produce a *total score* ranging from 400 to 1600. These are scaled scores, calculated by taking the number of right answers and converting them to the scaled score using a scoring table unique to the particular test the student took. This is done to ensure that differences in difficulty across forms will not affect scores. Note that students do not lose points for wrong answers.

Each student will also get three *Test Scores* in Reading, Writing and Language, and Mathematics ranging from 10 to 40. These scores are tied directly to the section scores: the EBRAW section score is the sum of the Reading and Writing test scores multiplied by 10. The Math section score is your Math test score multiplied by 20.

Each student will also get a variety of *subscores* for different types of questions within each section. These scores are either on a 1 to 15 or 10 to 40 scale. Students who take the essay will get three *essay scores*, each on a 2 to 8 scale. The essay scores are separate from the rest of the test; they will not be factored into students' EBRAW section scores or any other scores.

This book will focus on the ELA-relevant portions of the test—Evidence-Based Reading and Writing section, and the Essay. We will not be discussing the Mathematics sections.

Table 1.2 Reading and Writing Subscores

Name	Type	Scale	Sections
Words in Context	Subscore	1–15	Reading, Writing and Language
Command of Evidence	Subscore	1–15	Reading, Writing and Language
Standard English Conventions	Subscore	1–15	Writing and Language
Expression of Ideas	Subscore	1–15	Writing and Language
Analysis in Science	Cross-Test Score	10–40	Reading, Writing and Language, Math
Analysis in History/ Social Studies	Cross-Test Score	10–40	Reading, Writing and Language, Math

Reading

There will be 52 total passage-based questions over five passages with 10–11 questions each. These questions will present a short passage on a particular topic, followed by questions asking about what the passage says. One of the passages will be a *double passage*, in which two passages on a similar topic are presented, followed by questions discussing each passage individually or the relationship between the two.

Passage Types

The passages used for the SAT will be drawn from one of three content areas: *Fiction*, *History/Social Studies*, and *Science*. Only one of these categories is "literature" in the traditional sense. The majority of the passages will be nonfiction essays on a variety of topics.

But that's not to say that traditional literature won't appear. Fiction passages may be drawn from recent novels or from classic works of literature. Note that all fiction passages will be *prose* fiction: no drama and no poetry.

Table 1.3 Passage Topics From Two Practice Tests

Passage	Test 1	Test 2
1. Fiction	From Lydia Minatoya, *The Strangeness of Beauty*, 1999	From Charlotte Brontë, *The Professor*, 1857
2. History/Social Studies	An essay about the relationship between the perceived and actual value of gift-giving, 2008	An essay about the role of ethics in economic decisions, 2013
3. Science	From a paper by Watson and Crick about the structure of DNA, 1953	A double passage with two articles about the effects of electronic media on the brain, both from 2010
4. History/Social Studies	From Virginia Woolf, *Three Guineas*, 1938, about the role of women in English society	From Elizabeth Cady Stanton's address to the 1869 Women's Suffrage Convention
5. Science	A double passage with two articles about space mining, both from 2013	From an article about scientists studying undersea waves, 2014

For example, table 1.3 shows the topics and sources of the passages in the first two tests in *The Official SAT Study Guide*, a book of official tests published by the College Board. Note that the passage types are always in the same order.

As you can see, the passages come from a wide range of eras, with some passages taken from very modern sources and some much older. Published tests have had passages taken from as far back as the late eighteenth century.

The variety of different passage contents can affect a student's ability to easily understand a passage. However, it obscures the most important thing to keep in mind about the passages themselves: *students do not need any outside knowledge to do the questions*, other than an understanding of the English language. Students will not be tested on specific content of literary history, nor will they be expected to be familiar with any historical events or scientific principles discussed in the passages. All they need is the information in the passage itself. You do not need to be a historian or a scientist. You just need to be able to read.

The Great Global Conversation

The test specifications dictate that one of the history/social studies passages will belong to what the College Board calls "The Great Global Conversation". This simply means it will be a primary source document of historical importance "on a topic such as freedom, justice, or liberty". The examples they have provided are usually taken specifically from American history (like the Elizabeth Cady Stanton passage mentioned above), but they need not be specifically American (like the Virginia Woolf passage mentioned above).

Data Figures

Two passages, one science and one history/social studies, will contain one or more figures presenting data that is somehow relevant to the passage. These could be tables, bar graphs, scatterplots, or any kind of data visualization. There will be some questions asking students to analyze the information presented, draw conclusions, or connect it to the passage.

Here's an example of a data question, taken from A-List's *The Book of Knowledge:*

Figure 1.1 Sample Data Question

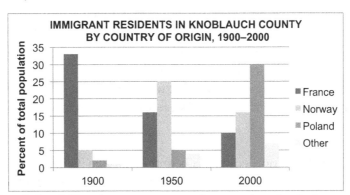

15. Which of the following statements is true for the information depicted in the graph?
A) The percentage of French residents was lowest in 1900.
B) The percentage of Norwegian residents peaked in 1950.
C) The percentage of Norwegian residents grew steadily over the years shown.
D) The percentage of Polish residents grew at a constant rate over the years shown.

Strategies

Main Ideas

One of the biggest problems students have with the passages is that reading takes a long time. Students try to memorize every point and understand every subtle detail and convoluted sentence in the passage. Instead, read the passage quickly and get the *main ideas*. Every paragraph is nothing more than a collection of sentences that have some common theme. That common theme is the main idea of the paragraph. It's the answer to this question: *What's it about?*

The goal is to *spend less time reading the passage* so you can spend *more time on the questions*, since the questions are what actually matters. Therefore, when reading the passage, skim the details and focus on the overall themes. These themes should be simple: the plot of the story, the argument of the essay, or the description of the information given. The details will become important only when and if a question asks about them.

Go Back to the Passage

Most questions will give a line reference saying exactly where in the passage the relevant information can be found. Once students read the question, before doing anything else, they should *go back to the passage and check the line reference*. If a question asks about line 35, go back to line 35 and see what it says before looking at the choices.

While students should not worry about the details when reading the passage, they can worry about the details once questions actually ask about them. The point is not to rely on what you remember about the passage. This is an open-book test. You can look it up.

Anticipate

All the information you need is in the passage itself. Read the question, follow the line reference back into the passage, and see what those lines say about the question. That's your *anticipation* of the answer to the question. Try to *paraphrase* the lines in your own word. The right answer will rarely be an *exact* match for the anticipation; rather, the right answer will have the same *meaning* as the anticipation, but worded differently. Then look at the choices and see which one matches the anticipation.

Eliminate

Sometimes it will be difficult to anticipate the answer based on the passage alone, but you can still eliminate choices that are obviously wrong and guess from what's left. Wrong choices are usually wrong for one of three reasons:

- ◆ **Random**. The choice talks about things that the passage doesn't even mention.
- ◆ **False**. The choice is explicitly contradicted by the passage.
- ◆ **Irrelevant**. The choice is something the author *says*, but it doesn't actually answer the question.

Note that all three of these reasons require you to have an understanding of what the passage does and doesn't say. But seeing that a wrong choice is wrong is often simpler than understanding the nuances of the correct answer. It's easier to spot a wrong choice than a right choice—after all, 75% of the choices are wrong.

Question Types

Passage questions tend to fall into easily recognizable types. These categories can give you a good sense of what the SAT expects you to be able to do.

- ◆ **Explicit questions** ask about what the passage literally states.

- **Evidence questions** ask students to choose which line from the passage provides evidence for the answer to a previous question.
- **Vocabulary-in-context questions** ask students to define a particular word as it is used in the context of a particular sentence in the passage.
- **Inferential questions** ask students to make conclusions about what the passage implies.
- **Main Idea questions** ask students to summarize or identify themes of part or all of the passage.
- **Strategy questions** ask about the author's rhetorical strategy or structural choices in the passage.
- **Tone questions** ask about the author's tone (or that of characters in a fiction passage).
- **Data questions** ask students to answer questions about a graph or table accompanying the passage, either on its own or in relation to the passage's contents.

Writing and Language

The Writing and Language test is composed of four short passages, each of which has 11 questions that ask about the grammar, usage, style, and rhetoric of the passage. The format is similar to the task of editing an essay: the student must make corrections to improve the essay, both in the context of an individual sentence its own right and in the larger context of the essay as a whole.

The passages will draw from four content areas: history/social studies, science, humanities, and careers. But the content of the passages has little impact on a student's ability to answer the questions. A question about proper comma placement will be the same regardless of what the sentence is about. One passage on the test will be accompanied by a graph or data representation, just like on the Reading test. There will be one or two questions that test students' ability to understand the figure. However, such questions will be a much smaller part of the Writing test than they were on the Reading test.

Students will get two subscores (1–15) in two main areas: **Standard English Conventions** (20 questions) and **Expression of Ideas** (25 questions).

Standard English Conventions

Standard English Conventions questions ask students to identify errors in a sentence. Generally, a word or part of a sentence will be underlined and students will be asked to choose how to rewrite the phrase according to rules of grammar, usage, and punctuation. Choice A) will usually be "NO CHANGE", meaning they can leave the phrase as it was originally written.

There are three types of Standard English Conventions questions:

- **Conventions of Usage**. These questions test relationships between single words and phrases within a sentence, relationships such as subject and verb, or pronoun and antecedent.
- **Sentence Structure**. These questions deal with the way larger parts of sentences are connected, such as the way to connect clauses properly and where to place long phrases.
- **Conventions of Punctuation**. These questions will usually present four choices that differ only in their punctuation. Students will be tested on when to use (and when not to use) commas, apostrophes, and other common punctuation marks.

Expression of Ideas

Expression of Ideas questions focus less on writing *grammatically* and more on writing *effectively*. It tests how to choose the best way to phrase a sentence, the best way to structure a paragraph, or the best way to accomplish the writer's goal. Unlike Standard English Conventions questions, Expression of Ideas questions may ask about the essay as a whole, not just single words or phrases.

There are three types of Expression of Ideas questions:

- **Effective Language Use**. These questions ask about the choice of language in the essay, as well as stylistic errors rather than grammatical or structural ones. Students will be asked to trim wordy sentences, make phrases more specific, or ensure the language accurately reflects the essay's tone.
- **Organization**. These questions ask about the logic and organization of the essay. Students will be asked about the location and ordering of sentences and the transitions between sentences or paragraphs.
- **Development**. These questions ask about what the author should do to the essay to improve it. In fact, most Development questions will explicitly phrase the question that way, asking what action the author should take. Common questions include whether the author should add or delete a sentence and whether the essay fulfills a certain goal. All questions dealing with figures and data are Development questions.

Essay

Format

The Essay will always be the last section of the SAT. It is optional, though if students do want to take it they must register for it in advance. While students are not required to take it, some colleges may require the SAT Essay when students send SAT scores.

The essay prompt will consist of a short passage, roughly the same length as a passage on the Reading test. These passages will be persuasive essays on a range in topics similar to those of the Reading test. Students will be asked to write an essay that describes and evaluates the author's persuasive strategies.

Every essay prompt will begin with this introduction before the passage:

> As you read the passage below, consider how [the author] uses
>
> ◆ evidence, such as facts or examples, to support claims.
> ◆ reasoning to develop ideas and to connect claims and evidence.
> ◆ stylistic or persuasive elements, such as word choice or appeals to emotion, to add power to the ideas expressed.

This is followed by a persuasive passage around 600–750 words long. Every prompt will have a version of this text after the passage:

> Write an essay in which you explain how [the author] builds an argument to persuade [his or her] audience that [the author's claim]. In your essay, analyze how [the author] uses one or more of the features listed in the box above (or features of your own choice) to strengthen the logic and persuasiveness of [his or her] argument. Be sure that your analysis focuses on the most relevant features of the passage. Your essay should not explain whether you agree with [the author's] claims, but rather explain how [the author] builds an argument to persuade [his or her] audience.

Students are given a maximum of four pages on which to write about the given topic. Essay readers understand that the essay is

About the SAT ◆ 13

intended as a first draft and the result will not be as polished as a school assignment would be.

Scoring

Students will receive grades in three different categories:

- ◆ **Reading**. How well does the student understand the content of the passage?
- ◆ **Analysis**. How well does the student analyze the author's rhetorical strategies and their effect?
- ◆ **Writing**. How well is the essay written?

The essay will be scored by two readers, each of whom will give it a score from 1 (bad) to 4 (good) in each of the three categories. If their scores in any one category differ by more than one point, the essay will go to a third reader to resolve the discrepancy. However, each reader may give disparate scores across the different categories. Thus, it is not permitted for one reader to give an essay a 2 in Reading and the other to give it a 4 in Reading. But it is permitted for one reader to give the same essay a 2 in Reading and a 4 in Analysis.

The final essay score will therefore consist of three scores from 2 to 8. The three scores are not combined into a single score, nor are they incorporated into any of the other scores for the EBRAW section.

Strategies

Students have 50 minutes for the essay, so they should have plenty of time to read the passage. Much like on the Reading test, students should write down the main idea of each paragraph in the margins. That way they'll be able to more easily understand the progression of the author's argument and identify where certain tactics were used.

When reading, students should be actively looking for those things mentioned in the prompt: the author's use of evidence, reasoning, and stylistic elements. Students should mention these elements in their main ideas to help them organize their thoughts. Students should think not only about *what* the author does in building their argument, but *why* and *how* they do it. That's what the Analysis score judges: students' ability to understand why the author made those choices.

Students should practice outlining and organizing their essays. Students should choose a thesis and explicitly state it. Paragraphs should be organized into discrete, coherent topics. This could be according to the chronology of the passage, according to the different persuasive elements used, or whatever the student finds most coherent.

Finally, practice essays should be reviewed together so students can begin to get a concrete sense of what effective and ineffective writing look like. Workshopping ideas, rereading past essays, and making revisions are all beyond the scope of a 50-minute essay, but they can help build the writing skills that students will need.

Changes to the Test

The SAT went through a well-publicized redesign, beginning with the PSAT in October 2015 and the SAT in March 2016. Ultimately, since the pre-2016 test is dead, it doesn't matter what the changes were; all that matters is what the test looks like now. But it's worth taking a quick look at those changes because (a) you may be more familiar with the older version of the test, and (b) examining what the College Board changed can help us understand their thinking about what they want the test to be.

Test Structure

- **Fewer sections**. The old test had ten sections, three in each subject plus a variable equating section in any subject. Each section was 25 minutes or less. The new test has fewer sections and more time per section.
- **Fixed section order**. The old test would mix up the order of the sections on each test administration so students wouldn't necessarily know what was coming next. The new test uses the same section order each time.
- **No equating section**. The old test contained one section that was used for setting the scoring table and did not count towards the student's score. The new test does not contain such a section.
- **No guessing penalty**. The old test subtracted a fraction of a point for each wrong answer in order to counteract the benefit of random guessing. The new test treats incorrect answers the same as blanks.
- **Fewer choices**. The old test had five choices for all multiple-choice questions. The new test has four.

Scoring

- **Two main scores**. The old test had three main scores, Reading, Math, and Writing, each scored from 200 to 800. The new test has two such scores, combining Reading and Writing into one 200–800 score.
- **More subscores**. The old test had (with the exception of Writing) no scores other than the main 200–800 scores. The new test has many additional subscores for all parts of the

16 ◆ About the SAT

test. A student's score report for the new test will contain 18 distinct scores in all.

Reading

- **Changed vocabulary emphasis**. One of the explicit goals of the redesigned Reading section was to remove the emphasis on defining esoteric words, instead emphasizing vocabulary in the context of a larger passage. The new test, therefore, no longer contains the vocabulary-centric Sentence Completion questions but has more Vocabulary-in-Context questions in the passages.
- **Passage content tweaked**. The old test contained passages in fiction, science, and history/social studies just like the new test does. The old test also contained passages in humanities, which have been removed from the new test. Additionally, the new test contains primary documents in "the Great Global Conversation" that were absent in the old test.
- **Increased passage complexity**. Both the old and the new test contained passages in a range of complexity. However, the new test seems to contain passages that are more difficult than those seen on the old test. This is compounded by the fact that the new test contains some passages that are older than what was on the old test, which rarely used texts from before the mid-nineteenth century.
- **New passage question types**. All question types that appeared on the old test continue to appear on the new test. However, the new test contains two types of questions— Evidence questions and Data questions—that did not appear on the old test.
- **Passages contain figures**. On the new test, two passages will be accompanied by graphs, tables, or other data representations. The old test had no such figures on the Reading sections.

Writing

- **Complete overhaul of format**. The Writing section on the old test featured questions of several different types, most of which were isolated sentences to be analyzed for grammatical mistakes. The new Writing test is entirely passage-based. It should be noted that this new format is almost identical to that of the ACT English test, which has been around for decades.

- **Less grammar, more rhetoric.** The old test, because of its single-sentence format, often tested rather complex and intricate constructions. While the new test fundamentally tests the same grammatical rules that the old test did, the questions and sentences themselves are more straightforward.
- **Skills beyond grammar.** With a few exceptions, the old Writing test was almost entirely about grammar and usage. The new test also includes questions about organization, development, and punctuation that were absent on the old test. It should be noted, again, that this makes the new test almost identical to the ACT English test.
- **Passages contain figures.** On the new test, one passage will be accompanied by graphs, tables, or other data representations. The old test had no such figures on the Writing sections.

Essay

- **Now optional.** The most obvious change is that the essay is now optional. In the old test, the essay was part of the Writing section and was always the first section of the test.
- **More time.** The old test allowed only a ridiculously short 25 minutes for the essay. The new essay gives a much more manageable 50 minutes.
- **New format.** The nature of the essay prompt is entirely different. The old test's essay was a broad, open-ended question that allowed students to write on almost any topic they wished. As such, it could be a persuasive, informative, or narrative essay. The new test is far more specific and asks students to analyze a given passage.
- **New scoring scale.** The old test used a holistic grading system that gave a single score from 2 to 12 for students' essays. This score was then factored into the 200–800 point Writing score. The new test's essay gives three scores from 2 to 8, which allows readers to judge different aspects of the essay separately.

2

Alignment With Common Core ELA Standards

How to Read the ELA Standards

The ELA standards are divided into strands (Reading, Writing, Speaking and Listening, Language). Each strand has a list of College and Career Readiness (CCR) anchor standards. These are the broad standards that students must attain in order to be deemed fit for college or a career beyond high school.

In addition, these standards are broken out for each grade level from kindergarten to grade 12, outlining what a student must be able to do and understand by the end of that grade level. For high school, standards are shown for two groupings, grades 9–10 and grades 11–12. Some grade-specific standards are further broken down into multiple subskills.

Some of these strands are also broken out into different content areas. For example, Reading has one set of anchor standards but has different grade-level standards for Reading Literature and Reading Informational Texts.

Each standard has a code containing three parts: letters denoting the strand or content area, the grade level of the standard or "CCR" for anchor standards, and the sequential number of the standard (sometimes with letters for subpoints). For example, "RL.CCR.5" refers to the fifth anchor standard in the Reading Literature strand, and "W.11-12.3a" refers to the first subskill of the third standard for the grade 11–12 standard in the Writing strand.

Alignment

In 2010, the College Board produced an alignment study to show how the standards aligned with the skills assessed by the old-format SAT. The results showed that the test significantly aligned with the standards.

Since then, the SAT has changed, of course, and the College Board has yet to produce a new alignment report. In order to determine alignment with the redesigned test, we used the initial alignment report and updated it according to what we know about the changes to the test. This includes the information the College Board has provided about the reasoning behind the redesign and specifications for the new test, along with the actual practice tests that have been released. The alignments provided here, then, are our own interpretation of how well the standards aligned, based on information and data from the College Board.

The following chart outlines the results for ELA standards, showing what percent of the standards in each strand align with each test's stated skill set.

Table 2.1 Alignment Summary

Common Core State Standard	Old SAT Alignment	Redesigned SAT Alignment
READING		
Reading Anchor Standards [R]	90%	100%
Reading Standards for Literature (11-12) [RL]	78%	78%
Reading Standards for Informational Text (11-12) [RI]	70%	100%
WRITING		
Writing Anchor Standards [W]	60%	50%
Writing Standards (11-12)	83%	70%
LANGUAGE		
Language Anchor Standards [L]	100%	100%
Language Standards (11-12)	67%	67%
Language Progressive Skills	94%	100%
Language Standards (11-12) and Progressive Skills	82%	86%

Certain ELA strands were not included in the College Board's original alignment report. These were excluded because they fell outside the scope of the old SAT. These standards do also show some alignment with the SAT—partly because of the redesign—but they will be excluded from this discussion. Those strands include:

- Reading Standards for History/Social Studies
- Reading Standards for Literacy in Science and Technical Subjects
- Writing Standards for Literacy in History/Social Studies, Science and Technical Subjects
- Speaking and Listening Standards and Anchor Standards

Some standards show what we call "partial alignment". In the SAT alignment report, certain standards that were shown as aligned had additional comments qualifying that alignment. The table shows percentages of standards that show any alignment; it does not distinguish partial and complete alignment.

How to Read This Section

The section is divided into four parts relating to the strands of the ELA standards:

- **Reading**. Ten anchor standards, with grade-specific standards in Literature and Informational Texts.
- **Writing**. Ten anchor standards, with grade-specific standards and multiple subskills.
- **Language**. Six anchor standards with grade-specific standards and multiple subskills. This section also reviews the Language Progressive Skills.
- **Other topics**. These topics are not discussed in detail because they are less directly relevant for SAT work and were not included in the College Board's alignment study.

Each section addresses each anchor standard, together with all its associated grade-specific standard for grades 11–12. Standards within each strand are usually organized into three or four groups of related concepts. (Please note that the headings listed for those groups come from the standards themselves, while the headings for the individual standards were written by A-List.)

The discussion of each standard is composed of several parts:

Table

Each anchor standard is shown in a table followed by the grade-specific standard for grades 11–12. Each table contains columns showing:

- The code for the standard, as defined by the CCSSI
- The standard itself
- Its alignment with the SAT

The two alignment columns will each display one of the following symbols:

- **Y** = The standard is aligned with the test in question.
- **N** = The standard is not aligned with the test in question.
- **P** = The standard is partially aligned with the test in question. For the SAT, this means a qualifying comment was listed for the standard.

If the standard aligns with a different subject than one would expect or with more than one subject of the test, then the letter of that subject will also be listed. For example, if a Reading standard aligns with an SAT Math skill, "YM" will be listed in the SAT column.

Alignment

Following the tables, we will briefly summarize the alignment with the CCR anchor standards and any grade-specific standards. If a standard is partially aligned—that is, the document considered it aligned, but with a qualification, or it only considered a portion of the standard to be aligned—we will list which segments do and do not align in the alignment section directly after the table.

Discussion

Here we discuss why and how the standards align and don't align. For those that don't align well with the test itself, we discuss how the standards might align to the skills and techniques used during the act of preparation. Furthermore, we discuss ways to incorporate material from the test into tasks beyond the scope of the test. Note the original alignment document often does not give detailed explanations about why a standard does or does not align with the test. Any discussion of such here is our own judgment based on our extensive experience and knowledge of the SAT.

Summary

We give a summary of the previous discussion. This summary may also list suggestions for how to use test material in ways beyond the test's scope in order to meet a standard that otherwise does not align.

Sample SAT Questions

When applicable, we provide a few sample questions that demonstrate the concepts discussed for that standard. The numbers given are three-part codes that show the practice test number, the section, and the question. For example, "3.1.24" refers to test 3, section 1, question 24.

Note that section 1 is always the Reading section and section 2 is always the Writing and Language section.

Three Levels of Alignment

Whether or not a standard aligns with the SAT is not always a simple question. There are three levels of alignment discussed in this document:

1. **Skills directly assessed by the test.** This is the substance of the alignment document prepared by the College Board itself and our subsequent update. The test already has its own list of skills that it measures directly. The skills needed for a student to meet each standard were compared to the skills students directly use when completing the test.
2. **Skills that are not assessed but are directly relevant.** These skills are not strictly necessary to answer the test *questions*, but they still are relevant to the act of test *preparation*. For example, Writing standard 5 says students should revise their writing, but the SAT Essay does not give students enough time to significantly revise their essays. However, in order to improve performance, it is vital that students review their essays after the test and figure out how it could have been better. Revision is a perfect way to do so.
3. **Skills that are beyond the scope of the test as written.** These skills clearly do not apply to the SAT. For example, several skills mention using technology or outside sources, both of which are not permitted on the ELA sections. However, teachers can still use and adapt the test material for larger assignments and projects that do align with these standards.

Alignment Beyond the Test

The amount of alignment relevant to you depends on your goal for your class. If you are simply teaching test preparation for the sake of doing well on the test, you should be concerned with the first-level alignment (the skills that are required to answer the questions) and the second-level alignment (the skills that will be needed during the test prep classroom activities). These skills alone account for the majority of the standards. This is an important point; you can be confident that *test prep is fully compatible with the Common Core*. Helping students to prepare for the test necessarily means helping students acquire and refine real skills they will need and use in college or careers.

Third-level alignment will not be relevant to test preparation, but test material needn't just be used for test preparation. These tests are a fertile raw material that can be adapted to fit your goals in your regular classes as well. For example, if you want to work on writing analytical essays, you can use practice SAT prompts to get started. These prompts have certain time, space, and other restrictions when given on the SAT, but you can use them in your classes however you wish, including for group collaboration, graphic or multimedia displays, or extensive research. If you are working to build reading comprehension skills for informative texts, but you don't have a ready supply of nonfiction texts, any practice SAT will have many nonfiction passages you can use to get started. Don't think of these tests as just tests; they are your own academic playgrounds.

Remember also that some standards will align poorly. The test will not perfectly satisfy all the Common Core requirements. Test preparation should not replace your usual English classes, but it can *supplement* them. Test prep gives you more reading drills, more writing exercises, more resources for grammatical instruction, all of it fully compatible with the standards. Not every standard aligns with the test, but every question on the test aligns with the standards.

26 ◆ Alignment With Common Core ELA Standards

Reading

Overview

The Reading strand is divided into four different content areas: Standards for Literature (RL), Standards for Informational Text (RI), Standards for Literacy in History/Social Studies (RH), and Standards for Literacy in Science and Technical Subjects (RST). All of these areas are tied to the same set of CCR anchor standards, but each has its own separate set of grade-specific standards (though many of these are similar to each other). The standards for history/social studies and science and technical subjects are not considered to be a part of the English Language Arts standards, so those will be discussed in a separate section.

There are ten CCR anchor standards for Reading. These are organized into four groups of similar concepts. Each section below lists the anchor standard followed by the grade-specific standard for grades 11–12 in Reading Literature and Reading Informational Text.

Each standard in this section is aligned against the Reading section, unless otherwise marked.

Here are a few notes about Reading before we get into the specifics:

♦ Virtually all of the Reading CCR anchor standards align with the SAT. The majority of the grade-specific standards in both Reading for Literature and Reading for Informational Texts align with the SAT. If you spend time preparing for the SAT, you can be confident you are helping students acquire and refine real skills they will need and use in college or careers.
♦ The test's passages use three content areas: fiction, history/social studies, and science. Generally speaking, the first area aligns with the Reading for Literature standards, while the other two align with the Informational Text standards. However, some of the nonfiction passages may still be historically important works that could be described as "literature", especially if, say, they are excerpts from a memoir or autobiography.
♦ There will be no poetry or drama on the SAT. That means that there will be no passages from Shakespeare. Any standards that specifically ask students to study Shakespeare are outside the scope of the test.
♦ Remember that these passages do not have to be used just for test prep. Any book of practice tests contains a virtual library of short passages on a wide variety of topics. You can have your students

read them without the questions; you can make up your own questions; you give a mini passage as a pop quiz if you have a few spare minutes in class; or you can look up the source of a passage and read a larger section of the original text. If you are doing serious test prep, you have to follow the test's rules, but if you're not, you can use the passages however you like. Be creative.

Key Ideas and Details

1. Read Closely

Code	Standard	Aligns
R.CCR.1	**Read closely to determine what the text says explicitly and to make logical inferences from it; cite specific textual evidence when writing or speaking to support conclusions drawn from the text.**	**Y**
RL.11-12.1	Cite strong and thorough textual evidence to support analysis of what the text says explicitly as well as inferences drawn from the text, including determining where the text leaves matters uncertain.	**Y**
RI.11-12.1	Cite strong and thorough textual evidence to support analysis of what the text says explicitly as well as inferences drawn from the text, including determining where the text leaves matters uncertain.	**Y**

Alignment

The SAT is aligned with the CCR Anchor and both grade-specific standards.

Discussion

What Aligns

The CCR Anchor matches perfectly with a primary goal of all reading passages. This is the essence of reading passages.

The most common question types ask students to find information explicitly stated by the passage, make inferences based on material stated by the passage, or provide evidence for a claim about the passage.

This standard perfectly describes three of the most common types of questions, which together make up over 40% of the Reading section. *Explicit questions* ask students to find information that is explicitly stated in the passage. *Inferential questions* ask students to make inferences based on material stated in the passage. *Evidence questions* ask students to provide textual evidence for their answers to previous questions, giving four possible line references.

That third question type is a new addition to the redesigned SAT. The College Board's alignment document for the old SAT included the comment, "The SAT does not require that students provide textual evidence. However, students must base inferences and analysis on the text provided in the passage or item stem." Now, however, not only does the test contain evidence questions as described above, these questions will contribute to the "Command of Evidence" subscore for the EBRAW section. It is likely that these questions were specifically added to the test to align it further with the CCSS.

For all questions on the Reading test, it's virtually impossible to discuss any of the material without backing up conclusions with evidence. All our reading strategies heavily rely on finding concrete evidence. Remember that these passages do not require any outside content knowledge other than vocabulary. That means all the needed information is right there in the passage.

The first rule of every passage question is to go back to the passage and find the information related to the question. When a question contains a line reference, it's inexcusable not to go back. Even in cases when the students cannot anticipate the answer simply by going back to the passage, they should be able to cite evidence to refute and eliminate the incorrect choices.

Even for questions that do not require students to cite specific evidence, it is crucial that students use evidence from the passages or sentences when choosing their answers. As teachers, you can and should demand that students justify all their choices with cited evidence.

Summary

Many, if not most, reading questions on the SAT ask students to determine what a text explicitly says or to make inferences based on the text. Some questions will explicitly ask students to cite evidence for their answers.

Sample SAT Questions

Explicit Questions: 1.1.13, 2.1.24, 3.1.12, 4.1.46

Inferential Questions: 1.1.26, 2.1.38, 3.1.3, 4.1.35

Evidence Questions: 1.1.14, 2.1.7, 3.1.4, 4.1.47

2. Central Ideas or Themes

Code	Standard	Aligns
R.CCR.2	**Determine central ideas or themes of a text and analyze their development; summarize the key supporting details and ideas.**	**Y**

(Continued)

30 ◆ Alignment With Common Core ELA Standards

Code	Standard	Aligns
RL.11-12.2	Determine two or more themes or central ideas of a text and analyze their development over the course of the text, including how they interact and build on one another to produce a complex account; provide an objective summary of the text.	**Y**
RI.11-12.2	Determine two or more central ideas of a text and analyze their development over the course of the text, including how they interact and build on one another to provide a complex analysis; provide an objective summary of the text.	**Y**

Alignment

The SAT is aligned with the CCR Anchor and both grade-specific standards.

Discussion

What Aligns

This standard directly addresses A-List's Main Idea strategy. Because of time constraints, students will not have enough time to read a passage as carefully as they might on their own. However, that doesn't mean they should ignore the passage entirely and jump right to the questions. On the contrary, it is important for them to have a sense of the overall story, information, or argument presented in the passage. Therefore, when students first encounter a passage, they should read the passage quickly, finding only the main ideas of each paragraph and of the passage as a whole.

There are several benefits to the Main Idea strategy beyond simple time management. First, by physically writing main ideas of each paragraph in the margins, students effectively produce a kind of outline of the passage. This will make it easier to find specific details if specific line references aren't given in a question.

Additionally, questions will often explicitly ask students for the main idea of a paragraph or the passage. Other times, knowledge of main ideas can help eliminate choices quickly. As we saw above, "Main Idea questions" was one of the primary question types for the SAT.

Summary

SAT questions frequently ask students to summarize or identify main themes of the passages. Additionally, finding the main ideas of a passage is a key strategy for all reading passages to help with time management, comprehension of the passage, and answering the questions.

Sample SAT Questions

Main Idea of the Passage: 1.1.1, 2.1.33, 3.1.21, 4.1.42

Main Idea of a Paragraph: 2.1.18, 2.1.42, 3.1.14, 4.1.11

3. Development and Interaction

Code	Standard	Aligns
R.CCR.3	**Analyze how and why individuals, events, and ideas develop and interact over the course of a text.**	**Y**
RL.11-12.3	Analyze the impact of the author's choices regarding how to develop and relate elements of a story or drama (e.g., where a story is set, how the action is ordered, how the characters are introduced and developed).	P
RI.11-12.3	Analyze a complex set of ideas or sequence of events and explain how specific individuals, ideas, or events interact and develop over the course of the text.	Y

Alignment

The SAT is aligned with the CCR Anchor and both grade-specific standards.

Discussion

What Aligns

This standard is to some extent a continuation of standard 2. The development of a text is closely related to the progression of its central themes. As such, finding main ideas of each paragraph and the passage as a whole will help understand this development much the same way it helps understand the progression of themes. This can be on a literal level of the setting, events, or actions described, or on a more abstract level of the ways and reasons that ideas change over the course of the text.

This standard has an additional component of how "the author's choices" relate to the development of the text. This concept will be actively tested on both the SAT. *Strategy questions* are those that ask about the author's choices and tactics in the construction of the text. For example, these questions can ask about why the passage was ordered a certain way, how one section relates to the passage as a whole, or what rhetorical strategies the author employs. But Strategy questions aren't the only type of questions that are relevant to this standard; Inferential questions, Main Idea questions, and even Explicit questions can deal with the development and interaction of ideas, too.

What Doesn't Align

The SAT does not align with the Literature standard's mention of "drama", since drama is excluded from the reading passages. All passages will be in prose. The College Board's study made no note of this in its study, however, and considered the test fully aligned.

Summary

Finding the main ideas in a passage can help students identify how the events and ideas develop throughout the text. Strategy questions ask how and why an author makes particular choices in the structure and development of the text.

Sample SAT Questions

Strategy Questions: 1.1.2, 2.1.3

Main Idea Questions: 3.1.11, 4.1.43

Craft and Structure

4. Meaning of Words

Code	Standard	Aligns
R.CCR.4	**Interpret words and phrases as they are used in a text, including determining technical, connotative, and figurative meanings, and analyze how specific word choices shape meaning or tone.**	**Y**
RL.11-12.4	Determine the meaning of words and phrases as they are used in the text, including figurative and connotative meanings; analyze the impact of specific word choices on meaning and tone, including words with multiple meanings or language that is particularly fresh, engaging, or beautiful. (Include Shakespeare as well as other authors.)	**Y**
RI.11-12.4	Determine the meaning of words and phrases as they are used in a text, including figurative, connotative, and technical meanings; analyze how an author uses and refines the meaning of a key term or terms over the course of a text (e.g., how Madison defines faction in Federalist No. 10).	**Y**

Alignment

The SAT is aligned with the CCR Anchor and both grade-specific standards.

Discussion

What Aligns

This skill is most prominently seen in *Vocabulary-in-Context questions*. These questions ask for the meaning of a specific word as it is used in a specific instance in the passage. For these questions, it is not enough for students to know the meaning of the word; they must also look at the context of the sentence. Vocabulary-in-Context questions often use common words in uncommon senses. In fact, these questions usually have incorrect distractor choices that could be valid definitions of the word in other contexts. These questions will contribute to the "Words in Context" subscore on the EBRAW section.

One of the changes of the redesigned SAT was to deemphasize difficult "SAT words" that were the hallmark of the old Sentence Completions section, which emphasized being able to explicitly define words. The new test instead focuses on words used in the context of the passage. Vocabulary-in-Context questions are not new—they have been a part of the test for decades—but they now appear with greater frequency than they did before.

The SAT also asks questions about tone. *Tone questions* might ask for the tone of a single word, a paragraph, or the entire passage. They even might ask to compare the tone of one passage in a double passage to the other. Often these questions can simply be done by determining whether the tone is positive, negative, or neutral, but sometimes students will need to be more particular.

What Doesn't Align

SAT Reading is not terribly concerned with "language that is particularly fresh, engaging, or beautiful". While the test does ask about the color and tone of the language an author uses, the test does not ask students to make *value judgments* about the passage. Students do not have to like the passage; they just have to understand it. Questions about whether a passage is "beautiful", then, fall outside the scope of the Reading test.

However, the Essay does ask students to write about the rhetorical strategies and effectiveness of a given passage, to analyze "stylistic or persuasive elements, such as word choice or appeals to emotion, to add power to the ideas expressed". In this task, then, students should absolutely "analyze the impact of . . . language that is particularly fresh, engaging, or beautiful."

Since drama is outside the scope of the test, the SAT would not use selections from Shakespeare in a reading passage, as mentioned in the Literature standard. However, the Informational Text standard is fair game, as primary historical documents such as the Federalist papers may be used as passages.

Summary

The test will ask questions about the specific meaning of a word in a specific context in the passage. The test will also ask questions about the tone of words or sections of a passage. The Reading test does not ask students to judge the beauty of words, but the Essay prompt may.

Sample SAT Questions

Vocabulary-in-Context Questions: 1.1.3, 1.1.45, 2.1.16, 2.1.37, 3.1.28, 3.1.35, 4.1.9, 4.1.34

Alignment With Common Core ELA Standards ◆ 35

5. Structure of Texts

Code	Standard	Aligns
R.CCR.5	**Analyze the structure of texts, including how specific sentences, paragraphs, and larger portions of the text (e.g., a section, chapter, scene, or stanza) relate to each other and the whole.**	**Y**
RL.11-12.5	Analyze how an author's choices concerning how to structure specific parts of a text (e.g., the choice of where to begin or end a story, the choice to provide a comedic or tragic resolution) contribute to its overall structure and meaning as well as its aesthetic impact.	**Y**
RI.11-12.5	Analyze and evaluate the effectiveness of the structure an author uses in his or her exposition or argument, including whether the structure makes points clear, convincing, and engaging.	**Y**

Alignment

The SAT is aligned with the CCR Anchor and both grade-specific standards.

Discussion

What Aligns

Structural questions such as these show up in the *Strategy questions* mentioned for standard 3 above. Strategy questions are those that ask about the author's choices and tactics in the construction of the text. For example, these questions can ask why the passage was ordered a certain way, how one section relates to the passage as a whole, or what rhetorical strategies the author employs.

Finding main ideas can also help identify quirks in the structure of the passage. Once students write down the main ideas for each paragraph, they will have a neat outline of the passage in the margins of the page. Examining the progression of ideas in that outline will help them see how different sections of the passage relate to each other to form the larger narrative or argument. Main Idea questions, which ask directly about the main ideas of the passage, often also relate these themes to the overall structure and development of the passage.

What Doesn't Align

The Reading test does not align well to the portion of the Information Text standard referring to "effectiveness" for the same reason that it did not align to the mention of "beauty" in standard 4 above. The test does not ask

36 ◆ Alignment With Common Core ELA Standards

students to make value judgments or decide whether the author's argument is persuasive. All they must do is determine what the author's argument says.

However, as mentioned in standard 4, the optional essay will require students to evaluate the effectiveness of a given passage's argument. While the essay prompt specifically asks students not to write whether they agree with the prompt, they are expected to analyze the different strategies the author employs in making the argument. Understanding the relative effectiveness of the strategies can be a useful part of understanding why the author constructed the passage as it is.

Summary

The test will ask questions about how and why an author makes particular choices in the structure and development of the text. Finding the main ideas in a passage can help students identify how the different sections of the text relate to each other and to the passage as a whole. The Reading test generally does not ask students to evaluate the effectiveness of an argument, but they can do so on the Essay.

Sample SAT Questions

Strategy Questions: 1.1.2, 1.1.46, 2.1.3, 2.1.28, 3.1.21, 4.1.23

6. Point of View and Purpose

Code	Standard	Aligns
R.CCR.6	**Assess how point of view or purpose shapes the content and style of a text.**	**Y**
RL.11-12.6	Analyze a case in which grasping point of view requires distinguishing what is directly stated in a text from what is really meant (e.g., satire, sarcasm, irony, or understatement).	**Y**
RI.11-12.6	Determine an author's point of view or purpose in a text in which the rhetoric is particularly effective, analyzing how style and content contribute to the power, persuasiveness, or beauty of the text.	**Y**

Alignment

The SAT is aligned with the CCR Anchor and both grade-specific standards.

Discussion

What Aligns

The point of view or purpose of a text is frequently an explicit topic of questions. Those that ask about the purpose of a text are usually categorized as Main Idea questions since they deal with the overall themes and content of the passage. Indeed, writing main ideas can help students understand purpose and point of view better. Main ideas seek to distill the content of a paragraph to a single sentence or phrase. But this needn't just be the content of the paragraph; it can and should include elements of the purpose of a paragraph, such as whether the author is giving an objective description or making an argument. The purpose of a passage is often directly related to the type of text it is—narrative, informative, or persuasive—so it can be useful for students to be able to recognize these distinctions.

Even when not specifically addressed in the question, identifying the purpose or point of view of the passage can be key to comprehension. For example, questions that ask about the tone of the passage often hinge on the distinction between actively condemning an unpleasant event and objectively describing it.

We've also already seen how Strategy questions can identify the choices that an author makes in constructing the text. One element of these choices is the decision to use certain rhetorical devices, such as irony or understatement. Such devices are explicitly tested on the SAT.

What Doesn't Align

The SAT Reading does not align with this Informational Text standard for the same reasons we saw for standards 4 and 5. The test does not ask students to make a value judgment or decide whether the author's argument is effective, persuasive, or beautiful. But all those things are central to the task of the Essay: to read a given passage and analyze how the arguments were constructed and why.

Summary

The point of view, purpose, and rhetorical devices employed in a passage are all material that is explicitly tested on the SAT Reading test and on the SAT Essay.

Sample SAT Questions

Purpose of a Paragraph: 1.1.7, 2.1.15, 2.1.43, 3.1.11, 3.1.48

Purpose of the Passage: 1.1.32, 2.1.11, 4.1.22, 4.1.41

Integration of Knowledge and Ideas

7. Diverse Formats and Media

Code	Standard	Aligns
R.CCR.7	**Integrate and evaluate content presented in diverse formats and media, including visually and quantitatively, as well as in words.**	**Y**
RL.11-12.7	Analyze multiple interpretations of a story, drama, or poem (e.g., recorded or live production of a play or recorded novel or poetry), evaluating how each version interprets the source text. (Include at least one play by Shakespeare and one play by an American dramatist.)	**N**
RI.11-12.7	Integrate and evaluate multiple sources of information presented in different media or formats (e.g., visually, quantitatively) as well as in words in order to address a question or solve a problem.	**Y**

Alignment

The SAT is aligned with the Anchor Standard and the Informational Text standard. The SAT is not aligned with the Literature standard.

Discussion

What Aligns

The old SAT Reading section was entirely text-based, so these standards did not align well (though they did align with certain questions in the Math section). However, one of the more prominent changes to the test was the addition of tables, graphs, and other data representations to both the Reading and Writing tests. Data questions ask students to be able to read and interpret the figure or figures. Sometimes these questions can be answered purely by looking at the figures, while other times they may require students to synthesize the information in the figures with the content of the passage. The addition of such figures was likely directly influenced by standards such as this one.

This skill also aligns with the SAT Math sections, which also sometimes require students to interpret data visualizations in the context of a setting.

What Doesn't Align

While the SAT does ask students to evaluate information in different "formats", that's not the case with presentations in other "media". The test will only be offered on paper: there will be no digital, audio, or video components.

The Literature standard does not align because the test will not contain any poems or drama. However, this grade-specific standard is a fairly narrow application of the CCR anchor standard, and there are other ways to apply the anchor to works of literature.

For comparison, consider the standard for grades 9–10. RL.9-10.7 states: "Analyze the representation of a subject or a key scene in two different artistic mediums, including what is emphasized or absent in each treatment (e.g., Auden's "Musée des Beaux Arts" and Breughel's *Landscape with the Fall of Icarus*)." This is still unaligned with the SAT, but it shows more clearly how test material can be expanded beyond its intended scope to include this standard. For example, a class can take a passage from a practice test and conduct research to find other texts across different media that address the same topic in different ways. These texts can include print sources like periodicals, and web sources like blogs, news sites, videos, or podcasts.

The point is that just because the test itself is limited to print media does not mean that your class discussion has to be. Reading passages can be springboards into a wide array of topics for conversation, research, and analysis.

Summary

Alignment
The SAT Reading includes passages accompanied by visual and quantitative figures, and questions will ask students to synthesize information in the figures with information in the passage. The test will not contain poetry or drama.

Beyond Alignment
Reading passages do not appear in varied media, but passages can be used for additional projects that delve into other media.

Sample SAT Questions
Data Questions: 1.1.20, 1.1.28, 2.1.19, 2.1.51, 3.1.20, 3.1.51, 4.1.19, 4.1.51

8. Evaluate Arguments

Code	Standard	Aligns
R.CCR.8	**Delineate and evaluate the argument and specific claims in a text, including the validity of the reasoning as well as the relevance and sufficiency of the evidence.**	**Y**
RL.11-12.8	(Not applicable to literature)	—

(Continued)

Code	Standard	Aligns
RI.11-12.8	Delineate and evaluate the reasoning in seminal U.S. texts, including the application of constitutional principles and use of legal reasoning (e.g., in U.S. Supreme Court majority opinions and dissents) and the premises, purposes, and arguments in works of public advocacy (e.g., The Federalist, presidential addresses).	**Y**

Alignment

The SAT is aligned with the CCR anchor standard and the Informational Text standard.

Discussion

What Aligns

This standard focuses on the argument and reasoning of a passage. Not all passages on the test are persuasive texts. However, those that are often have questions about the strength and logic of the argument. For example, a question may ask, "Which of the following, if true, would weaken the author's argument?" This does not require the student to actually take a position, but it does require the student to determine what facts would or would not affect the logical force of the argument.

These types of issues show up particularly frequently on Data questions. Passages that have accompanying figures will often ask about how the figures relate to the author's claims, particularly whether they support particular claims. They also show up often on SAT double passages. Often the two passages will present opposing sides of an issue. One passage will directly address the argument presented in the other, and questions ask students to identify how the authors respond to each other's evidence.

These issues also appear on the Essay. The prompt presents a persuasive essay and specifically asks students to write an essay to "explain how [the author] builds an argument to persuade [his or her] audience." The essay is not intended to argue for or against the author's point, but it would certainly require the student to "delineate and evaluate the argument".

The College Board's alignment document listed the Informational Text standard as not aligned because the old SAT did not contain "seminal U.S. texts". However, one of the changes in the redesign was to include such texts as reading passages. The test still does not require outside knowledge of history, so questions won't delve too deeply into the realm of "legal reasoning", but certainly students may be asked to evaluate the reasoning and arguments of such documents.

Summary

The SAT may include questions evaluating the force and logic of an argument when persuasive texts appear as passages (particularly on double passages). Seminal U.S. texts may appear as passages. The SAT Essay requires students to analyze an argument of a given passage.

Sample SAT Questions

Argument: 1.1.50, 2.1.12, 3.1.41, 4.1.36

Data Questions: 1.1.29, 2.1.21, 3.1.52, 4.1.52

9. Multiple Texts

Code	Standard	Aligns
R.CCR.9	**Analyze how two or more texts address similar themes or topics in order to build knowledge or to compare the approaches the authors take.**	**P**
RL.11-12.9	Demonstrate knowledge of eighteenth-, nineteenth-, and early-twentieth-century foundational works of American literature, including how two or more texts from the same period treat similar themes or topics.	**N**
RI.11-12.9	Analyze seventeenth-, eighteenth-, and nineteenth-century foundational U.S. documents of historical and literary significance (including The Declaration of Independence, the Preamble to the Constitution, the Bill of Rights, and Lincoln's Second Inaugural Address) for their themes, purposes, and rhetorical features.	**Y**

Alignment

The SAT is aligned with the CCR Anchor Standard. The alignment document included the note, "The SAT does not require students to compare more than two texts." The redesigned SAT is aligned with the Informational Text standard but not the Literature standard.

Discussion

What Aligns

The CCR Anchor standard aligns very well with the SAT double passages, the point of which is to analyze how two texts address similar themes and to compare the authors' approaches.

Each SAT will have one double passage. Double passages will present two passages on similar or overlapping themes. Understanding the connection between the two authors' arguments or perspectives is often crucial to double passage questions. The relationship between the passages may be as simple as the pro and con sides of an argument, or they can be more subtle variations of each other. Every double passage will always be followed by at least some questions that ask to relate the two passages together. Students should expect this and look to understand the overlap between passages as they first read them. Questions may also ask about differences in tone, form, or rhetorical strategies of the two passages.

The old SAT was not aligned with the Informational Text standard, but the redesigned SAT is. As was mentioned previously, foundational texts of American history do appear on the redesigned SAT. Questions about "themes, purposes, and rhetorical features" are certainly likely to appear.

What Doesn't Align
The SAT is not well aligned with the Literature standard for two reasons. First, the double passage on the Reading test will be in science or history/social studies, not fiction, so the test will not ask students to compare two pieces of fiction. Now, while the foundational documents that appear are classified as history/social studies, one could argue that they fall into the realm of literature (certainly if authors like Virginia Woolf and Edmund Burke are included). However, the second problem is that students are not required to "demonstrate knowledge" of these texts. All questions will only require the information that is in the passage; students will not be required to have any existing knowledge of the texts presented.

Summary
The SAT reading section contains a double passage with questions asking students to compare and contrast the texts. The SAT will contain American foundational documents. The double passage will not be fiction. The test does not require any existing knowledge of history or literature.

Sample SAT Questions
Double Passage Questions: 1.1.49, 1.1.52, 2.1.31, 2.1.32

Founding Documents Double Passage Questions: 3.1.40, 3.1.38, 4.1.38, 4.1.41

Range of Reading and Level of Text Complexity

10. Text Complexity

Code	Standard	Aligns
R.CCR.10	**Read and comprehend complex literary and informational texts independently and proficiently.**	**Y**
RL.11-12.10	By the end of grade 11, read and comprehend literature, including stories, dramas, and poems, in the grades 11–CCR text complexity band proficiently, with scaffolding as needed at the high end of the range. By the end of grade 12, read and comprehend literature, including stories, dramas, and poems, at the high end of the grades 11–CCR text complexity band independently and proficiently.	**Y**
RI.11-12.10	By the end of grade 11, read and comprehend literary nonfiction in the grades 11–CCR text complexity band proficiently, with scaffolding as needed at the high end of the range. By the end of grade 12, read and comprehend literary nonfiction at the high end of the grades 11–CCR text complexity band independently and proficiently.	**Y**

Alignment

The SAT is aligned with all three standards along with the comment: "Passages for the SAT are chosen by a process that considers complexity and grade-level appropriateness."

Discussion

Text complexity was a major concern in the development and creation of the Common Core State Standards. Studies had found a wide gap between the complexity level of texts read in high school and those read in the first year of college—a gap that actually has been widening over time.

The SAT has always gone to great lengths in selecting the appropriate passages to use for their reading sections. While individual passages will vary in their complexity and difficulty, the overall reading level of the passages is appropriate for grades 11 to 12.

One of the main changes to the Reading test has been to reevaluate the complexity of texts chosen. The design specifications for the new test say texts are aligned "with the requirements of first-year college courses and workforce training programs" and that they are "challenging but not inaccessible to college- and career-ready test-takers" ["Test specifications for the redesigned SAT", p. 26]. Overall, this meant increasing the complexity of some passages on the new test as compared with the old test.

On the other hand, one of the great advantages of spending time preparing for the test is that even students with poor reading skills can substantially improve their performance on difficult, complex texts. The nature of the test is such that students do not need to have a complete understanding of a passage in order to do well on the questions. Through a combination of finding main ideas, going back to the passage, anticipating, and eliminating, students can drastically cut down on the amount of work they need to put into a passage. Large chunks of a passage can be ignored because no questions ask about it. Difficult questions can be done easily, because, while the correct answer involves subtle understanding of the passage, the wrong answers can be eliminated quickly.

It may seem that these kinds of techniques and preparation run counter to the spirit of the standards, that this is a way to use tricks to answer the questions without actually improving reading skills. But that is not the case at all. On the contrary, these techniques are simply the first step in showing students that complex passages that seem impenetrable are in fact perfectly comprehensible. Low-scoring students with poor reading skills are often frightened by the prospect of reading long passages. This fear can fester because students do not realize how much they already understand, how much they are already capable of doing. A-List's techniques directly work to counter this fear.

What does this mean for the classroom? The basics of the techniques' focus on reducing the amount of work students must do. If your only concern is test preparation, you can stop there. But if you want to continue to push students' reading skills, you can continue to discuss passages and questions long after all the answers have been found. Even though this paragraph is never mentioned in the questions, talk about how it relates to the rest of the passage. Even though you've eliminated all the wrong answers, keep discussing a question until students understand why the correct answer is correct. The techniques are a starting point, not an end point.

And, of course, there is certainly no shortage of questions that require a nuanced understanding of a difficult passage. Students aiming for the highest scores on the test will have to read closely and carefully in order to get the most difficult questions. The test is long enough that you can tailor the same material to the whole spectrum of ability. You can adjust your demands to match your students' skills to make sure that every student is pushed to the edge of his or her potential.

Summary

Alignment
SAT passages are chosen so as to be appropriately complex for grades 11–12, while also aligned with the requirements for first-year college courses. For struggling students, many test-taking techniques aim to simplify otherwise complex texts.

Beyond Alignment
For struggling students, the test is flexible enough that classroom activities can be adjusted to match the appropriate reading level for your students.

46 ◆ Alignment With Common Core ELA Standards

Writing

Overview

There are ten CCR anchor standards for Writing. These are organized into four groups of similar concepts. Each section below lists the anchor standard followed by the grade-specific standard for grades 11–12. For most of the standards, the grade-specific standards are broken down into a number of distinct but related skills.

Since these standards are about actual writing production, they are aligned here against the skills associated with the essay, not those associated with the multiple-choice Writing and Language questions. Alignment with the Essay is marked with an "E" and alignment with the Writing and Language is marked with a "W". The multiple-choice sections will be addressed further in the Language strand.

The majority of the Writing standards do align well. If you spend time preparing for the test, you can be confident you are helping students acquire and refine real skills they will need and use in college or careers.

It may seem as if the SAT deemphasizes essay writing since it is an optional section. If you are running a test prep course, you may find yourself spending less time on the essay and more time on the Writing test. That's fine; those questions are important and also align with the Core Standards. But feel free to spend more time on writing essays if you want additional work on honing students' writing skills beyond what is necessary for the test. The prompts are excellent exercises both inside and outside the confines of the test.

Here are some options for how to treat the essays:

- For test prep classes, you can assign them as the test intends under time constraints, as part of a full practice test, or in a separate timed session for the essay alone.
- Outside test prep classes, you can give them as stand-alone homework assignments to practice writing on a small scale.
- For anyone, you can workshop outlines and review practice essays in small or large groups.
- Outside test prep classes, you can push them well beyond the intended short time and space constraints, into longer essays, multimedia presentations, or even research projects.

Remember also that the format of the Writing and Language section mimics the act of editing an essay: removing commas, correcting verbs, reordering sentences, etc. Reviewing student essays, therefore, can be excellent preparation for the multiple-choice questions as well.

Text Types and Purposes

The three anchor standards in this section address the three main types of essays students should be able to write—*persuasive, informative,* and *narrative.* The grade-level standards then apply parallel subskills to each of the types.

In general, the *SAT aligns well with persuasive and informative essays but not with narrative essays.* The prompt for the SAT Essay asks students to read a passage, then describe and analyze the author's argument and rhetorical strategies. This fits well with standards asking students to write persuasive essays (the student will have a thesis about the passage that must be defended) and informative essays (the students should accurately describe what the passage says and does). However, it is not well suited for narrative essays: students should address the given essay, not write fiction or describe personal events.

Each of the Anchor Standards has subskills that are roughly parallel in what they address:

- ◆ 1a, 2a, and 3a address the establishment of the essay's topic.
- ◆ 1b, 2b, and 3b address the essay's development.
- ◆ 1c, 2c, 2d, and 3c address the language and sentence structure.
- ◆ 1d, 2e, and 3d address the style and tone.
- ◆ 1e, 2f, and 3e address the conclusion of the essay.

All of these, in general, align to the SAT Essay. All are explicitly mentioned in the College Board's scoring rubric for essay scoring, most of which contribute to the "Writing" component of the Essay score.

It should also be noted that many of these skills (particularly c, e, and f) are also explicitly tested in the multiple-choice Writing and Language questions, which can contain persuasive, informative, and narrative passages.

1. Write Arguments

Code	Standard	Aligns
W.CCR.1	**Write arguments to support claims in an analysis of substantive topics or texts, using valid reasoning and relevant and sufficient evidence.**	**YE**
W.11-12.1a	Introduce precise, knowledgeable claim(s), establish the significance of the claim(s), distinguish the claim(s) from alternate or opposing claim(s), counterclaims, reasons, and evidence.	**YE**

(Continued)

Code	Standard	Aligns
W.11-12.1b	Develop claim(s) and counterclaims fairly and thoroughly, supplying the most relevant evidence for each while pointing out the strengths and limitations of both in a manner that anticipates the audience's knowledge level, concerns, values, and possible biases.	**YE**
W.11-12.1c	Use words, phrases, and clauses as well as varied syntax to link the major sections of the text, create cohesion, and clarify the relationships between claim(s) and reasons, between reasons and evidence, and between claim(s) and counterclaims.	**YWE**
W.11-12.1d	Establish and maintain a formal style and objective tone while attending to the norms and conventions of the discipline in which they are writing.	**YE**
W.11-12.1e	Provide a concluding statement or section that follows from and supports the argument presented.	**YW**

Alignment

The SAT is aligned with the CCR and all the grade-specific standards. All standards are aligned with skills required for the essay, but standards 1c and 1e are also aligned with skills required for the multiple-choice Writing questions.

Discussion

The SAT Essay prompt is not constructed as a traditional two-sided argument, but it does require the skills involved in writing persuasive essays. The test requires students to develop and maintain a strong point of view. It requires students to use appropriate examples and evidence from the source passage to support the position. It requires students to show facility in language, use a variety of sentence structures, and write mostly free of grammatical and mechanical errors. All of these elements strongly align with the standards listed here.

The multiple choice Writing questions feature questions about word choice, syntax, and tone that align well with standard 1c. Standard 1e aligns better with the Writing test than with the essay. While the essay certainly allows students to write conclusions, it does not require them. The Writing test, however, will sometimes feature questions that specifically ask for effective conclusions to the passage.

Summary
The SAT Essay requires the skills involved in writing persuasive essays. It requires a clear point of view, evidence or examples, and sophisticated, varied language. The SAT Writing asks about word choice, syntax, and concluding paragraphs.

2. Write Informative Texts

Code	Standard	Aligns
W.CCR.2	**Write informative/explanatory texts to examine and convey complex ideas and information clearly and accurately through the effective selection, organization, and analysis of content.**	**YE**
W.11-12.2a	Introduce a topic; organize complex ideas, concepts, and information so that each new element builds on that which preceded it to create a unified whole; include formatting (e.g., headings), graphics (e.g., figures, tables), and multimedia when useful to aiding comprehension.	**PE**
W.11-12.2b	Develop the topic thoroughly by selecting the most significant and relevant facts, extended definitions, concrete details, quotations, or other information and examples appropriate to the audience's knowledge of the topic.	**YE**
W.11-12.2c	Use appropriate and varied transitions and syntax to link the major sections of the text, create cohesion, and clarify the relationships among complex ideas and concepts.	**YWE**
W.11-12.2d	Use precise language, domain-specific vocabulary, and techniques such as metaphor, simile, and analogy to manage the complexity of the topic.	**YE**
W.11-12.2e	Establish and maintain a formal style and objective tone while attending to the norms and conventions of the discipline in which they are writing.	**YE**
W.11-12.2f	Provide a concluding statement or section that follows from and supports the argument presented (e.g., articulating implications or the significance of the topic).	**YW**

Alignment

The SAT is aligned with the CCR Anchor and all the grade-specific standards. In the alignment document, standard 2a included the comment, "Formatting and multimedia are not applicable to the SAT." All standards are aligned with skills required for the Essay, but standard 2c is also aligned with skills required for the multiple-choice Writing questions.

Discussion

This standard addresses informative essays, in which the author simply describes a situation, concept, or series of events.

What Aligns

The SAT Essay is well positioned for writing an informative essay. Since the focus of the prompt is to explain how the author builds an argument in the passage, the student must lay out the content of the passage clearly and explicitly. The Anchor standard here is almost a perfect description of the student's task with respect to the passage.

All the points mentioned for standard 1 apply equally to standard 2. The test requires students to develop and maintain a strong point of view. It requires students to use appropriate examples and evidence from the passage to support the position. It requires students to show facility in language, use a variety in sentence structure, and write mostly free of grammatical and mechanical errors. Standard 2c and 2f are also aligned with the multiple-choice Writing questions, which specifically ask about word choice, syntax, and conclusions.

What Doesn't Align

Standard 2a does not fully align with the SAT Essay. Because they are handwritten and given over short time periods, any sort of formatting, graphics, or multimedia presentations would not be possible. However, such elements can certainly be included if topics from the test are used for longer assignments or research projects outside of test prep.

Summary

Alignment

The SAT Essay prompt is well structured for writing an informative expository essay. The essay requires a clear point of view, evidence or examples, and sophisticated, varied language.

Alignment With Common Core ELA Standards ◆ 51

Beyond Alignment
Neither essay permits electronic formatting or visual aids, but such elements can be included if topics are used for longer projects outside of test prep.

3. Write Narratives

Code	Standard	Aligns
W.CCR.3	**Write narratives to develop real or imagined experiences or events using effective technique, well-chosen details, and well-structured event sequences.**	**N**
W.11-12.3a	Engage and orient the reader by setting out a problem, situation, or observation and its significance, establishing one or multiple point(s) of view, and introducing a narrator and/or characters; create a smooth progression of experiences or events.	**N**
W.11-12.3b	Use narrative techniques, such as dialogue, pacing, description, reflection, and multiple plot lines, to develop experiences, events, and/or characters.	**N**
W.11-12.3c	Use a variety of techniques to sequence events so that they build on one another to create a coherent whole and build toward a particular tone and outcome (e.g., a sense of mystery, suspense, growth, or resolution).	**N**
W.11-12.3d	Use precise words and phrases, telling details, and sensory language to convey a vivid picture of the experiences, events, setting, and/or characters.	**YW**
W.11-12.3e	Provide a conclusion that follows from and reflects on what is experienced, observed, or resolved over the course of the narrative.	**YW**

Alignment

The SAT Essay is not aligned with the CCR Anchor standard or any of the grade-specific standards. The SAT Writing test is aligned with standards 3d and 3e.

Discussion

This standard addresses narrative essays, which tell a coherent story or set of experiences, either fictional or true.

This is one of the only places where the redesigned test is *less* aligned with the CCSS than the old test was. The old SAT Essay featured an open-ended prompt that allowed students to write nearly any sort of essay they wished, be it persuasive, informational, or narrative, and the College Board's alignment document described it as such. The new format, however, has a very narrow topic, asking students to write a specific type of analysis on a specific passage. This does not lend itself well to writing narratives of any kind.

The skills listed still align with the SAT generally with the sort of writing students must produce, but here in the context of a narrative they are not aligned.

The Writing test, however, may contain narrative passages. Like we've seen on the previous two standards, questions on these standards may ask about word choice (standard 3d) or about concluding paragraphs (standard 3e).

Summary

The redesigned SAT Essay is not well structured for writing narratives. The Writing test may contain narrative passages with questions that align with some of these standards.

Alignment With Common Core ELA Standards ◆ 53

Production and Distribution of Writing

4. Clear and Coherent Writing

Code	Standard	Aligns
W.CCR.4	**Produce clear and coherent writing in which the development, organization, and style are appropriate to task, purpose, and audience.**	**YE**
W.11-12.4	(Grade-specific expectations for writing types are defined in standards 1–3.)	—

Alignment
The SAT is aligned with this standard.

Discussion

What Aligns
This standard is essentially a combination of the first three (as is evidenced by the note referring to grade-specific standards 1–3). The goal of any of these essays is to produce clear and coherent writing. As we saw in each of the first three standards, all of the grade-specific standards specifically addressed the development, organization, and style of the essays, as well as adhering to a clear and specific purpose.

Summary
The SAT Essay requires students to produce clear and coherent writing and to be attentive of their essays' development, organization, and purpose.

5. Revise and Strengthen Writing

Code	Standard	Aligns
W.CCR.5	**Develop and strengthen writing as needed by planning, revising, editing, rewriting, or trying a new approach.**	**PWE**
W.11-12.5	Develop and strengthen writing as needed by planning, revising, editing, rewriting, or trying a new approach, focusing on addressing what is most significant for a specific purpose and audience. (Editing for conventions should demonstrate command of Language standards 1–3 up to and including grades 11–12.)	**PWE**

Alignment

The SAT Essay and multiple-choice sections are aligned with both the CCR and the grade-specific standard. The alignment study included the note: "The SAT does not measure a student's ability to plan or try a new approach."

Discussion

What Aligns

As we've said, the essay is intended to be a first draft written in a short period of time. With 50 minutes allotted, students will have some time to outline, reread, or revise the draft, but not very much.

However, while the essays cannot be revised much during the test, the skills involved in revising and strengthening one's writing are very much apparent in the multiple-choice section. The SAT Writing test is set up to mimic the process of editing a finished draft, making necessary revisions for grammar, style, and coherence. The test is composed of four passages on a variety of topics. The questions attached to the passage take two basic forms: a word or phrase in the passage is underlined and students must choose the best word or phrase to go in that spot, attending to the grammar, style, and punctuation of the sentence; or, the question will ask whether a certain revision—such as moving, inserting, or deleting a phrase or sentence—should be made and why. Both of these formats represent the sort of questions students should ask themselves when reviewing their own writing.

The parenthetical note in the grade-specific standard refers to the "Progressive Skills" discussed in the Language strand.

What Doesn't Align

As we said, because of time limits, major revision is not within the scope of the essay on the test itself. However, while you can't revise very much during the test, editing, revision, and discussion can be very prominent parts of your preparation for the test. This is a *second-level alignment*. Look at essays that students wrote under time constraints for practice tests and discuss what makes them strong and what needs improvement. Discuss ways of improving these essays with the class as a whole. The better students understand how to make their writing strong, the easier it will be for them to make it strong in the first place, during real test conditions.

Furthermore, you can expand your work on the essays beyond the scope of the test. Use the prompts from the tests to make longer assignments. Have students workshop their essays together. Have them revise those essays in depth to make complete, refined second drafts. These activities clearly go beyond what the test requires of them, but can still be valuable tools to strengthen their writing skills.

Summary

Alignment
The essay's time limit is too short to permit serious revisions, but the multiple-choice section is designed to mimic the act of revising a piece of writing.

Beyond Alignment
The writing assignments can also be expanded to assignments that produce more polished drafts.

6. Use Technology

Code	Standard	Aligns
W.CCR.6	**Use technology, including the Internet, to produce and publish writing and to interact and collaborate with others.**	**N**
W.11-12.6	Use technology, including the Internet, to produce, publish, and update individual or shared writing products in response to ongoing feedback, including new arguments or information.	**N**

Alignment

The SAT is not aligned with either the CCR Anchor or the grade-specific standard. The document includes a note that reads, "The use of technology is beyond the scope of the SAT."

Discussion

The test does not permit the use of any technology (with the exception of calculators, which are allowed only on one of the Math sections). Clearly, this standard is beyond the scope of basic preparation for the test.

However, teachers can use test material to give assignments beyond the scope of the test in order to incorporate technology. We mentioned in the discussion of standard 5 above that teachers can continue essay writing assignments beyond the first draft to incorporate more editorial revision. Such assignments can also incorporate technology in different ways. For example, students can write their essays on computers and exchange drafts via email to critique each other's writing. Or students can create blogs in which they post drafts of their essays, and classmates can discuss them in the comments below. These projects can last a week or can continue throughout a semester.

Summary
The SAT does not permit the use of technology on the essay, but teachers can use the essay prompts to come up with new assignments that use computer or Internet technology to revise and strengthen their writing.

Research to Build and Present Knowledge

7. Conduct Research

Code	Standard	Aligns
W.CCR.7	**Conduct short as well as more sustained research projects based on focused questions, demonstrating understanding of the subject under investigation.**	**N**
W.11-12.7	Conduct short as well as more sustained research projects to answer a question (including a self-generated question) or solve a problem, narrow or broaden the inquiry when appropriate; synthesize multiple sources on the subject, demonstrating understanding of the subject under investigation.	**N**

Alignment
The SAT is not aligned with either the CCR Anchor or the grade-specific standard. The document includes a note that reads, "The element of research is beyond the scope of the SAT."

Discussion
Like standard 6, this standard in itself does not align at all to the test, but it can align with additional tasks that push beyond the intended scope of the test. The essay is intended to be a first draft written in a short period of time, and students will not have access to research material during the test. Given more time and space, however, students can greatly expand their discussions, and research can be a central element of this work.

For example, the passages that the students are asked to analyze are all persuasive essays arguing a particular position. Students can research the issue discussed and try to find additional perspectives on the same issue. Given the prompt's emphasis on analyzing rhetorical strategies, they can find other examples of people making the same argument using different strategies, or the opposing argument using the same strategies, or whatever their research finds. They can place the issue in a broader historical context. While the prompt asks them not to take a side on the issue, in a longer project, they can and should. There are many possibilities for expanding the breadth of the task.

Summary
Extended research is beyond the scope of the SAT, but teachers can use the essay prompts as the basis for extended research projects.

8. Use Multiple Sources

Code	Standard	Aligns
W.CCR.8	**Gather relevant information from multiple print and digital sources, assess the credibility and accuracy of each source, and integrate the information while avoiding plagiarism.**	**N**
W.11-12.8	Gather relevant information from multiple authoritative print and digital sources, using advanced searches effectively; assess the strengths and limitations of each source in terms of the task, purpose, and audience; integrate the information into the text selectively to maintain the flow of ideas, avoiding plagiarism and overreliance on any one source and following a standard format for citation.	**N**

Alignment
The SAT is not aligned with either the CCR Anchor or the grade-specific standard. The document includes a note that reads, "The element of gathering information from multiple sources is beyond the scope of the SAT."

Discussion
This standard is a natural extension of standard 7 discussed above. Like standard 7, this standard in itself does not align at all to the SAT, but it can align with additional tasks pushed beyond the intended scope of the test.

As discussed earlier, the essay can be used as the basis of extended research projects. When assigning such projects, students can be required to use multiple print and digital sources. In so doing, they can analyze each source to assess its strengths and limitations and integrate the information into their own work. Their searches for this material lend themselves to classroom discussions about the reliability of information and how to assess a text's authority and accuracy.

Summary

Beyond Alignment
Extended research is beyond the scope of the SAT, but teachers can use the essay prompts as the basis for extended research projects. These research projects can draw on multiple print and digital sources and analyze their strengths and limitations.

9. Use Literary or Informational Texts

Code	Standard	Aligns
W.CCR.9	**Draw evidence from literary or informational texts to support analysis, reflection, and research.**	**PE**
W.11-12.9a	Apply grades 11–12 Reading standards to literature (e.g., "Demonstrate knowledge of eighteenth-, nineteenth-, and early-twentieth-century foundational works of American literature, including how two or more texts from the same period treat similar themes or topics").	**PE**
W.11-12.9b	Apply grades 11–12 Reading standards to literary nonfiction (e.g., "Delineate and evaluate the reasoning in seminal U.S. texts, including the application of constitutional principles and use of legal reasoning [e.g., in U.S. Supreme Court Case majority opinions and dissents] and the premises, purposes, and arguments in works of public advocacy [e.g., The Federalist, presidential addresses]").	**YE**

Alignment

The SAT is aligned with both the CCR Anchor and the grade-specific standards.

Discussion

What Aligns

These standards relate back both to the research discussed in standards 7 and 8 above and to the grade-specific standards discussed for the Reading strands. Standards 7 and 8 ask students to write research projects that include multiple outside sources. The CCR Anchor here asks students to include literature or literary nonfiction as sources. The grade-specific standards then demand that students treat those texts as we described in the strands for Reading Literature and Reading Informational Texts. (The examples quoted in the grade-specific standards above are RL.11-12.9 and RI.11-12.8, respectively, but all of the RL and RI grade-specific standards apply here.)

As stated before, actual research and use of multiple sources are outside the scope of the essays on the test. However, these standards actually align well with the SAT Essay on its own terms. The whole point of the prompt is to use a given source. That source passage looks just like a Reading test passage, and students should approach them the same way, focusing on finding main ideas for each paragraph.

60 ◆ Alignment With Common Core ELA Standards

As such, students are absolutely expected to draw evidence from texts to support analysis. The entire point is to do so. Similarly, all the standards for Reading Literature and Reading Informational Texts that aligned with the Reading test also align here to the essay.

What Doesn't Align

The Anchor standard mentions "research" which, again, is not in the scope of the test. The Reading Informational Texts standards all aligned to the SAT, but not all the Reading Literature standards did. Thus, alignment with 9a here is marked as partial.

Summary

The SAT Essay requires students to use examples to analyze and draw evidence from a given text. This text will be similar to those described in the Reading strands, so all standards that were aligned before continue to be aligned here.

Range of Writing

10. Write Routinely

Code	Standard	Aligns
W.CCR.10	**Write routinely over extended time frames (time for research, reflection, and revision) and shorter time frames (a single sitting or a day or two) for a range of tasks, purposes, and audiences.**	**P/N**
W.11-12.10	Write routinely over extended time frames (time for research, reflection, and revision) and shorter time frames (a single sitting or a day or two) for a range of tasks, purposes, and audiences.	**P/N**

Alignment

The SAT is not aligned with this standard. The alignment document includes a note that reads, "The SAT aligns with writing over 'shorter time frames' only." The comment included in the SAT document implies that this standard is partially aligned, but the study considered it unaligned in computing the percentages in the summary table. This is why we marked the standard in the table as both partially aligned and not aligned.

Note that the grade-level standard is identical to the CCR Anchor standard.

Discussion

Obviously, the essay only permits writing over a short time frame (specifically: 50 minutes). Writing routinely and writing over extended time frames do not fall within the scope of the test.

However, one way to use test material to write routinely is to *do a lot of practice tests*. This is a second-level alignment. The College Board provides practice tests on their website. One of the biggest difficulties in writing these essays is dealing with the time limit. If you are preparing your students for the SAT, they should be sure to practice writing these essays as often as possible before the test. Writing these essays routinely is highly recommended.

Additionally, as we mentioned before, students can go back and review their essays outside of the time constraints of the test. This is an incredibly useful exercise; probably the most effective way of becoming a better writer is to review and revise your work. Certainly, it is necessary for improving performance on the SAT Essay.

Furthermore, as we've already seen several times in the standards discussed above, the prompts can be applied to other projects beyond the constraints of the test. This is a third-level alignment. Think of the essay prompts as raw materials that can be used on their own merits or as jumping-off points for larger assignments. These assignments can be individual or group projects; they can be expositions or extensive research projects; they can be tightly timed or stretched over weeks. There are many ways the prompts can be used, depending on what kind of skills you want to foster and strengthen in your students.

Summary

Each individual essay is intended to take a short period of time, but students should review and revise their essays after the test is over and should practice by going through multiple prompts on a regular basis. Extended writing is beyond the scope of the SAT, but teachers can use the essay prompts as the basis for longer projects.

Alignment With Common Core ELA Standards ◆ 63

Language

Overview

The Language strand is the intersection of the Reading and Writing strands. Reading standards ensure students can comprehend entire texts; Writing standards ensure they can produce them. Language standards focus instead on the more elementary parts of texts—the words, the sentences, and the structures that lie beneath them.

There are six CCR anchor standards for Language. These are organized into three groups of similar concepts. Each section below lists the anchor standard followed by the grade-specific standard for grades 11–12. For most of the standards, the grade-specific standards are broken down into a number of distinct but related skills.

(Technical note: for every standard in this strand, there is *one* main grade-specific standard for grades 11–12, which may then also have some subskills associated with it. Most of the time, the grade-specific standard is identical to the CCR Anchor, so we did not bother to list the main grade-specific standard, only the subskills. For example, L.CCR.1 is associated with L.11-12.1 (not shown), which is identical to L.CCR.1 but distinct from L.11-12.1a and L.11-12.1b. There is one exception to this template: L.11-12.4 below is similar but not exactly identical to L.CCR.4. Note that the SAT document only conducted alignment with the CCR and the subskills, not the main grade-specific standards like L.11-12.4.)

Additionally, the last section here will discuss the Progressive Skills standards. So far, this document has focused on the grade-specific standards for grades 11–12, but remember that the standards cover every year from kindergarten onwards. The grade-specific standards show what students in a particular grade should be learning with respect to the CCR, but they also presuppose that they've already learned a large swath of material earlier. When talking about something like the rules and conventions of grammar and usage, one often composes lists of the various rules that students need in order to be competent and fluent in the language. According to the standards' template, students will acquire those rules slowly over the course of their entire schooling. The Progressive Skills list outlines what these rules are and when students are expected to learn them.

(Of course, that doesn't mean your students actually will have done so. You may have to introduce them to concepts that, in the future when the standards are fully implemented, they should have learned in third grade.)

Because these language standards appear in several different areas of the test, when a standard partially or fully aligns with the SAT, the tables below will list the letters of any and all subjects that the standard aligns with: Reading (R), Writing (W), Math (M), and Essay (E).

Conventions of Standard English

1. Grammar and Usage

Code	Standard	Aligns
L.CCR.1	**Demonstrate command of the conventions of standard English grammar and usage when writing or speaking.**	**YWE**
L.11-12.1a	Apply the understanding that usage is a matter of convention, can change over time, and is sometimes contested.	**N**
L.11-12.1b	Resolve issues of complex or contested usage, consulting references (e.g., *Merriam-Webster's Dictionary of English Usage, Garner's Modern American Usage*) as needed.	**N**

Alignment

The SAT Writing is aligned with the CCR Anchor standard. The SAT is not aligned with either of the grade-specific standards.

Discussion

What Aligns
The CCR Anchor is an excellent summary of the entire purpose of the SAT Writing and Essay. Effectively employing the rules and conventions of standard written English, whether that be in reviewing sentences and passages provided by the test or producing one's own writing, is obviously the central focus of these sections (though there is no speaking part on either test).

What Doesn't Align
The two grade-specific standards here, however, do not align well with the test. The test requires students to be familiar with the major rules of grammar and usage, but these standards go further to involve a kind of metacommentary about what it means to be a rule of grammar and usage, how to determine whether something is a rule, and how these rules came to be. Certainly the test requires students to identify the arbitrary conventions of English, but if a student does not understand the nature of that convention, he or she can still get the questions right.

The grade-specific standards seem oddly different from the CCR Anchor here. Why not discuss some of those specific rules of grammar and usage, rather than this metacommentary? Remember, however, that the standards are a set of standards for all grades starting in kindergarten. The standards listed for grades 11–12 are the last piece of the grammatical puzzle, the apotheosis of a lifetime of grammatical studies. Yes, the standards expect students to be able to identify subject-verb agreement and shifts in verb tense, but they expect students to do so long before high school. See the "Progressive Skills" at the end of this chapter for a timeline of when students are expected to know various rules and conventions.

Issues regarding contested or evolving usage are outside the scope of the test; in fact, the test generally does a good job of avoiding such issues so that every question will have unambiguously correct and incorrect choices. That said, there are certainly contentious constructions, issues that can be confusing and muddled even for experienced teachers, such as use of singular "they" or what constitutes the appropriate use of passive or subjunctive verbs. The works cited in the standard (particularly *Merriam-Webster's Dictionary of English Usage*) are excellent sources for further discussions of these topics. Additionally, there are several great websites and blogs, such as *Language Log* or John McIntyre's *You Don't Say*, that discuss some of these issues regularly and in depth.

While not required, discussions about these complex issues can be quite fruitful in class discussions about grammar. Such conversations can help instill a deeper understanding of linguistic principles in the students. Granted, if working with a class that struggles with grammatical issues, it's often best to avoid these more intricate discussions simply because the students need as much time as possible on the rules themselves. But, to a certain extent, these conversations are unavoidable. Often students will ask "should I say *X* or *Y*?" and the answer will be more complex than a simple binary answer. Being aware of the histories of these constructions can lead to deeper understanding.

Summary

Alignment
The SAT Writing is almost entirely devoted to assessing students' knowledge of the conventions of standard written English. Students will be expected to use these conventions themselves on the essay.

66 ◆ Alignment With Common Core ELA Standards

Beyond Alignment
The test does not require students to have an understanding of complex, evolving, or contested usage, but conversations about them can be useful in instilling a deeper understanding of linguistic principles.

Sample SAT Questions
Conventions of Usage: 1.2.40, 2.2.41, 3.2.28, 4.2.6

2. Orthography

Code	Standard	Aligns
L.CCR.2	**Demonstrate command of the conventions of standard English capitalization, punctuation, and spelling when writing.**	**YWE**
L.11-12.2a	Observe hyphenation conventions.	**YE**
L.11-12.2b	Spell correctly.	**YWE**

Alignment
The SAT Writing is aligned with the CCR Anchor and the grade-specific standards.

Discussion
The word "orthography" often refers solely to the spelling of words, but it can also have a broader sense referring to any set of characters and symbols used in writing, including capitalization, hyphenation, and punctuation. The SAT specifically and frequently tests punctuation. There will be around six to eight Conventions of Punctuation questions on each Writing test, which solely test knowledge of proper punctuation. The four choices for a given phrase will be worded the same, differing only in punctuation. Additionally, there will be some grammatical issues that involve punctuation, such as avoiding comma splices.

Spelling will not be tested with regard to words that are difficult to spell (like "accommodate" or "conscience"). However, students will be asked to choose between commonly confused words (like "their" vs. "they're" or "to" vs. "too"), which is at heart a spelling issue.

Capitalization and hyphenation, in contrast, are not tested and will not be at issue on any questions. So why does the College Board consider L.11-12.2a to be aligned? Because the SAT Essay requires students' writing to be generally "free of most errors in grammar, usage and mechanics". Issues of spelling, punctuation, et al., belong to the realm of mechanics. An essay with a few spelling mistakes can still score highly, but when those mistakes start to add up, it impedes the essay's readability and it can affect the score.

Summary
Students are required to follow the rules of capitalization, spelling, punctuation, and hyphenation in their own writing on the essay. The multiple-choice questions raise issues of punctuation and spelling explicitly.

Sample SAT Questions
Spelling: 1.2.19, 2.2.38, 3.2.26, 4.2.30

Punctuation: 1.2.15, 2.2.14, 3.2.35, 4.2.22

68 ◆ Alignment With Common Core ELA Standards

Knowledge of Language

3. Style and Meaning

Code	Standard	Aligns
L.CCR.3	**Apply knowledge of language to understand how language functions in different contexts, to make effective choices for meaning or style, and to comprehend more fully when reading or listening.**	**YW**
L.11-12.3a	Vary syntax for effect, consulting references (e.g., Tufte's *Artful Sentences*) for guidance as needed; apply an understanding of syntax to the study of complex tasks when reading.	**YW**

Alignment

The SAT Writing is aligned with the CCR Anchor and the grade-specific standard.

Discussion

What Aligns
The SAT features questions of style most explicitly in Effective Language Use questions. For these questions, students don't pick the most *grammatical* phrasing, but the most *elegant* phrasing. Frequently, questions will feature choices containing phrases that do not violate any rules of grammar or usage but are wordy, redundant, or vague. Furthermore, because the Writing test is made up of long passages, questions also may ask for the choice that most closely matches a style or tone already established in the passage.

Students not only need to be able to identify effective writing, they also need to be able to produce it themselves. The essay requires students to write clearly, effectively, and elegantly in order to communicate their point. Being free of errors of grammar and usage is only one element of effective use of language, and students must be able to use their knowledge of syntax and style toward strengthening their own writing.

Understanding the function of language is also relevant to the reading sections. The Reading test often includes passages that contain tricky sections with complex sentence structures or common words applied to uncommon contexts. A deeper understanding of how these structures work and how meaning is shaped by context can be crucial to understanding what a passage is trying to say.

What Doesn't Align

Obviously, the reference to "listening" in the Anchor standard doesn't apply to the SAT. Additionally, the call to consult outside references is beyond the scope of the test itself, as outside texts are not permitted. But an understanding of the effect of syntax is a fundamental concept of effective writing that will be relevant to understanding any text students read and producing coherent texts of their own. Consulting outside references is considered a higher-level alignment, however, as additional sources can be used if essay prompts are stretched to longer assignments outside the scope of the SAT.

The grade-specific standard may seem a bit odd here, seemingly far removed from the Anchor's call to understand stylistic choices. But remember that this is the grades 11–12 standard. Students will be expected to acquire more basic stylistic skills in earlier grades, as shown in the Progressive Skills table later in this section.

Summary

The SAT requires students to be able to identify effective writing style on multiple-choice questions, produce effective writing in their essays, and understand complex structures in their readings.

Sample SAT Questions

Effective Language Use: 1.2.13, 1.2.33, 2.2.10, 2.2.19, 3.2.8, 3.2.23, 4.2.14, 4.2.16

70 ◆ Alignment With Common Core ELA Standards

Vocabulary Acquisition and Use

4. Determine the Meaning of Words

Code	Standard	Aligns
L.CCR.4	**Determine or clarify the meaning of unknown and multiple-meaning words and phrases by using context clues, analyzing meaningful word parts, and consulting general and specialized reference materials, as appropriate.**	**YR**
L.11-12.4	Determine or clarify the meaning of unknown and multiple-meaning words and phrases based on grades 11–12 reading and content, choosing flexibly from a range of strategies.	—
L.11-12.4a	Use context (e.g., the overall meaning of a sentence, paragraph, or text; a word's position or function in a sentence) as a clue to the meaning of a word or phrase.	**YR**
L.11-12.4b	Identify and correctly use patterns of word changes that indicate different meanings or parts of speech (e.g., conceive, conception, conceivable).	**N**
L.11-12.4c	Consult general and specialized reference materials (e.g., dictionaries, glossaries, thesauruses), both print and digital, to find the pronunciation of a word or determine or clarify its precise meaning, its part of speech, its etymology, or its standard usage.	**N**
L.11-12.4d	Verify the preliminary determination of the meaning of a word or phrase (e.g., by checking the inferred meaning in context or in a dictionary).	**YR**

Alignment

The SAT reading sections are fully aligned with the CCR Anchor standard and standards 4a and 4d. The SAT is not aligned with standards 4b or 4c. (Notice that here L.CCR.4 is not identical to L.11-12.4. For grade-specific standards that contain subskills, the SAT only included the subskills and the CCR Anchor in their alignment study.)

Discussion

What Aligns

This standard is similar to R.CCR.4, "Interpret words and phrases as they are used in a text, including determining technical, connotative, and figurative meanings, and analyze how specific word choices shape meaning or tone." Whereas that standard referred to interpreting the subtle differences in word meanings, this standard specifically refers to words whose meanings are unknown or that have multiple potential meanings.

Standard 4a closely describes the skill needed for Vocabulary-in-Context questions on the passage-based sections. These questions ask for the meaning of a specific word as it is used in a specific instance in the passage. For these questions, it is not enough for students to know the meaning of the word; they must also look at the context of the sentence. Vocabulary-in-Context questions may use unknown words or common words used with alternate, less common meanings. In fact, these questions usually have incorrect distractor choices that could be valid definitions of the word in other contexts. Standard 4d is relevant in this sense—students can guess the meaning of the word in isolation based on their existing knowledge of it, but must also verify its intended meaning in context.

What Doesn't Align

Standard 4b does not align with the SAT. This standard was not aligned with the old test, but frankly it's a bit strange that it's not now aligned with the new test. One of the most noticeable changes to the Writing section was to make it more similar to the ACT English test, both in format and in question types. The ACT does align with this standard, often asking students to select from multiple forms of a single word such as distinguishing parts of speech. Given the presence of this standard, one would think that the SAT might want to adopt those questions as well, but it's not listed among the skills tested, and no questions like this appear on any of the released practice material. Understanding word roots was more important on the old test when Sentence Completion questions often used more difficult or obscure words, but the importance of such words has been scaled back on the redesigned test.

Standard 4c does not align well within the scope of the SAT, since reference material is not permitted during the test. However, when reviewing practice material, we absolutely recommend students pick out all the words they did not know and physically look up their meanings in a dictionary to identify their meanings and alternate forms. In fact, A-List's suite of vocabulary materials includes several mechanisms that allow students to create their own lists of words: *The A-List Vocabulary Box* comes with blank flash cards, and *Vocab Videos* comes with an electronic flashcard generator, both of which can be used to add words to their existing vocabulary lists.

Summary

The SAT frequently requires students to determine or guess the meaning of unknown words on Vocabulary-in-Context questions, which ask about the specific meaning of a word in a specific context in the passage.

Sample SAT Questions

Vocabulary-in-Context questions: 1.1.3, 1.1.45, 2.1.16, 2.1.37, 3.1.28, 3.1.35, 4.1.9, 4.1.34

5. Figurative Language and Nuance

Code	Standard	Aligns
L.CCR.5	**Demonstrate understanding of figurative language, word relationships, and nuances in word meanings.**	**YR**
L.11-12.5a	Interpret figures of speech (e.g., hyperbole, paradox) in context and analyze their role in the text.	**YR**
L.11-12.5b	Analyze nuances in the meaning of words with similar denotations.	**YR**

Alignment

The SAT Reading section is aligned with the CCR Anchor and the grade-specific standards.

Discussion

As we've already seen, the SAT features Vocabulary-in-Context questions that test students' understanding of the intended sense of a word as it's actually used in a passage. The choices for these questions are often similar enough to each other that they demand a subtle understanding of the word and the sentence.

In fact, attention to nuance is important throughout the reading sections. Almost every question will contain choices that to the careless reader will sound similar to each other, and it requires a deeper understanding, either of the passage or of the choices, to be able to distinguish them properly.

Figures of speech are often present on reading passages. As we saw in our discussion in the Reading strand, Strategy questions are those that identify the choices that an author makes in constructing the text. One element of these choices is the decision to use certain rhetorical devices or figures of speech, such as irony, hyperbole, or paradox.

Summary

Figurative language appears and is explicitly tested on the SAT Reading test. Nuances of the meanings of words are important on Vocabulary-in-Context questions.

Sample SAT Questions

Word Choice: 1.2.1, 2.2.28, 3.2.40, 4.2.16

6. Learn More Words

Code	Standard	Aligns
L.CCR.6	**Acquire and use accurately a range of general academic and domain-specific words and phrases sufficient for reading, writing, speaking, and listening at the college and career readiness level; demonstrate independence in gathering vocabulary knowledge when considering a word or phrase important to comprehension or expression.**	**PRW**
L.11-12.6	Acquire and use accurately a range of general academic and domain-specific words and phrases sufficient for reading, writing, speaking, and listening at the college and career readiness level; demonstrate independence in gathering vocabulary knowledge when considering a word or phrase important to comprehension or expression.	**PRW**

Alignment

The CCR Anchor standard is identical to the grade-specific standard. The SAT is aligned with the standard with the following comment: "The SAT measures the use of accurate vocabulary, not acquisition."

Discussion

The changes to the SAT over the past 30 years have shown a steady elimination of questions that require students to explicitly define words: in 1994 the test cut the antonyms section, in 2005 the analogies, and now in 2016 the sentence completions. Each of these sections were made up of questions for which rote memorization could benefit students. Now this steady pruning has reached its conclusion, and the reading sections are entirely made up of passage-based questions.

The rhetoric surrounding the latest redesign frequently emphasizes this elimination of "irrelevant words", focusing instead on words that you will encounter in real life, words that, according to their website "you will probably encounter in college or in the workplace long after test day". This, frankly, is insulting. The sentence completions featured difficult words, surely, but they were hardly obscure. Nearly all the vocabulary that appeared there were words that could regularly be found in well-respected print sources like *The New York Times*.

Secondly, the new SAT has some crazy-hard words in it. Here are the correct answers on some of the hardest Sentence Completion questions on the free sample of the old SAT: *discern*, *indulged*, *apportionment*, *circumscribed, simplistic, prodigious.* Here are some words that appear in passage 4 of practice test 1: *vantage, pulpit, trapesing, venerable, caravanserai.* I ask you, do you often encounter the word "caravanserai" in your workplace? (I suppose I do, but my job involves doing passage 4 on practice test 1.)

Mocking the test is fun, but they do have a point about the shift in vocabulary focus. The test still has hard words on it; the difference is that the words only appear in the context of a larger passage. Questions like sentence completions on the old SAT would effectively ask students to know the dictionary definition of words. Which is hard! It's even hard to define words whose meaning you already know.

But again, *the test still has hard words on it.* Having a wide and diverse vocabulary is a crucial element to success on the Reading section. Reading passages are often dense and difficult to read, and having a rich vocabulary is important to understanding them.

Additionally, some questions, like the Vocabulary-in-Context questions we've already seen, will explicitly ask students to define words. But these won't be difficult words—they're more likely to be relatively easy words that have multiple meanings, so you must use the context of the passage to determine which meaning is being used.

The note in the alignment document makes a good point: from the test's perspective, the act of acquisition is irrelevant. Even though the College Board has explicitly stated that one goal of the redesign is to end flashcard cramming, the test itself is agnostic about how students came to know a word, whether through their own outside reading, through dedicated study of vocabulary words, or through cramming the night before the test. All that matters is whether students know a word.

Of course, as we can see above, alignment with this standard goes well beyond the Reading test. Vocabulary is an important component to every section:

♦ On the Writing test, students must understand how specific words relate to each other, such as the nuances in meaning that dictate the best word to choose for a sentence or idiomatic rules dictating which preposition must follow a verb.
♦ On the Essay, similar issues of word choice and vocabulary are very much in play. Proper and sophisticated use of language is one of the key areas upon which essays will be judged.
♦ Even the Mathematics sections expect students to know the definitions of key mathematical terms such as "integer" or "slope". All subjects involve some reading, and all reading is inseparably linked to vocabulary.

Summary

Alignment

The SAT demands that students know and use vocabulary in a variety of subjects: reading passages use sophisticated words and questions ask about their nuances, multiple-choice grammar questions ask about proper word choice, and the essay demands sophisticated vocabulary.

The test does not demand any particular method of vocabulary acquisition, but many students will need to study vocabulary in some way.

Progressive Skills

Code	Skill	Aligns
L.3.1f	Ensure subject–verb and pronoun–antecedent agreement.	**Y**
L.3.3a	Choose words and phrases for effect.	**Y**
L.4.1f	Produce complete sentences, recognizing and correcting inappropriate fragments and run-ons.	**Y**
L.4.1g	Correctly use frequently confused words (e.g., to/too/two; there/their).	**Y**
L.4.3a	Choose words and phrases to convey ideas precisely. (Subsumed by L.7.3a.)	—
L.4.3b	Choose punctuation for effect.	**Y**
L.5.1d	Recognize and correct inappropriate shifts in verb tense.	**Y**
L.5.2a	Use punctuation to separate items in a series. (Subsumed by L.9-10.1a.)	**Y**
L.6.1c	Recognize and correct inappropriate shifts in pronoun number and person.	**Y**
L.6.1d	Recognize and correct vague pronouns (i.e., ones with unclear or ambiguous antecedents).	**Y**
L.6.1e	Recognize variations from standard English in their own and others' writing and speaking, and identify and use strategies to improve expression in conventional language.	**P**
L.6.2a	Use punctuation (commas, parentheses, dashes) to set off nonrestrictive/parenthetical elements.	**Y**
L.6.3a	Vary sentence patterns for meaning, reader/listener interest, and style. (Subsumed by L.11-12.3a.)	**Y**
L.6.3b	Maintain consistency in style and tone.	**Y**
L.7.1c	Place phrases and clauses within a sentence, recognizing and correcting misplaced and dangling modifiers.	**Y**
L.7.3a	Choose language that expresses ideas precisely and concisely, recognizing and eliminating wordiness and redundancy.	**Y**

(Continued)

Code	Skill	Aligns
L.8.1d	Recognize and correct inappropriate shifts in verb voice and mood.	**Y**
L.9-10.1a	Use parallel structure.	**Y**

Alignment

The SAT Writing section is aligned with all Progressive Skills standards. Standard L.4.3a was not included in the alignment table (presumably because it's subsumed by standard L.7.3a, which aligns with the test).

Discussion

What Aligns

The standards are made up of two components: the CCR anchor standards give the broad overall skills that students will ultimately need for success in college or a career, and the grade-specific standards that detail what aspect of those skills should be acquired by a given year. As we mentioned at the beginning of this chapter, this book focuses on the grade-specific standards for grades 11–12, since that's when students take the SAT, but the standards cover every year from kindergarten onwards. The grade-specific standards show what students in a particular grade should be learning, but they also presuppose that they've already learned a large quantity of material earlier.

The table above outlines the component concepts and skills that students will need to acquire in order to meet CCR Anchor standards by the end of high school.

The codes for each standard adhere to the same system the standards always use. The "L" means this is a standard in the Language strand. The first number shows the grade by which the standard should be met. The standards listed here start in grade 3 and run up to grades 9–10. The second number shows the CCR Anchor standard to which the specific standard corresponds. All standards here correspond to Language standards 1, 2, or 3.

Note that the letters that follow the standard number are unique to that grade level's standards. Standard L.5.2a ("Use punctuation to separate items in a series.") is the first subpoint for the fifth grade under Language CCR Anchor 2; it is connected to L.CCR.2 ("Demonstrate command of the conventions of standard English capitalization, punctuation, and spelling when writing."), but has no particular relationship to skill 2a for other grades (such as L.11-12.2a, "Observe hyphenation conventions.").

These skills go as far back as third grade, but that doesn't mean they aren't relevant for 11th and 12th graders. The key word here is *progressive*; students should acquire each new skill in the order listed above, but they should also retain all the knowledge and skills acquired in previous years so that they can build up to more and more complex ideas. This is why the 11–12 grade-specific skill for standard 1 discussed above involved the meta-commentary about complex and contested usage—such discussions are only possible after having spent a great deal of time reviewing all the nuts and bolts of the grammar.

As for the content of these progressive skills, they couldn't be better suited for the SAT. Every skill listed here will in some form be a part of the test. The old SAT was not aligned with L.4.3b, but punctuation is now a larger part of the redesigned Writing test, so it aligns fully. If one were to devise a list of rules that are tested on the multiple-choice sections of the SAT Writing, this would be a perfect template. Subject-verb agreement, pronoun-antecedent agreement, fragments, run-ons, tense, parallelism—it's as if the CCSSI created the standards directly out of A-List's *The Book of Knowledge*. Take a look at a couple of practice questions from the book:

Once a reliable method for measuring degrees of longitude [1] <u>were discovered</u>, cartographers were able to draw accurate maps of the oceans.	**1.**	A) NO CHANGE B) discovers C) was discovered D) would have discovered
Douglas hates using his debit card, believing that someone could easily steal it and gain access to his [2] <u>account, he prefers</u> using cash whenever he can.	**2.**	A) NO CHANGE B) account. He prefers C) account he prefers D) account. Preferring

Question 1 has choices dealing with subject–verb agreement, tense, and voice. Question 2 has choices dealing with run-ons, fragments, and punctuation. Between two questions, we have addressed five standards.

What Doesn't Align
Only one item here does not perfectly align with the test: Standard L.6.1e only partially aligns, excluding the reference to speaking (obviously) and the phrase "identify and use strategies to improve expression in conventional language". But both of these standards can be applied to students' own writing on the essays.

Summary

The Progressive Skills table is a veritable checklist of the grammatical rules and skills that are tested on the SAT. Virtually every one is prominent on the Writing test.

Sample SAT Questions

Here is but a sample of the above skills appearing on the SAT:

Subject–verb Agreement: 1.2.40

Frequently Confused Words: 4.2.30

Punctuation for a Series: 1.2.4

Vague Pronouns: 2.2.5

Dangling Modifiers: 4.2.43

Word Choice: 2.2.36

Punctuation: 1.2.26

Shifts in Pronoun Number and Person: 1.2.44

Punctuation for Parenthetical Elements: 1.2.15

Redundancy: 3.2.18

Fragments: 3.2.14

Verb Tense: 1.2.18

Parallel Structure: 3.2.19

Other Topics

Reading, Writing, and Language are the three main strands of the English Language Arts standards, but there are a few other strands that we have not discussed. They were excluded from our main discussion because the College Board's own alignment study excluded them, often because they were so poorly aligned that discussing them would distract from the segments that align well.

But that does not mean you should ignore them altogether. As we've seen many times, even standards that are beyond the intended scope of the test can be met by stretching and adapting test material.

The excluded strands include:

- Two content areas in the Reading strand: **Reading Standards for Literacy in History/Social Studies (RH)** and **Literacy in Science and Technical Subjects (RST)**. These ten grade-specific standards correspond to the ten CCR Anchor standards for Reading.
- One content area in the Writing strand: **Writing Standards for Literacy in History/Social Studies, Science, and Technology (WHST)**. These ten grade-specific standards correspond to the ten CCR Anchor standards for Reading.
- An additional strand, **Speaking and Listening (SL)**. The tables show six new CCR anchor standards and six associated grade-specific standards.

The SAT excluded all of these strands from the 2010 study with the following note:

The Speaking and Listening Standards are best addressed through classroom performance tasks and teacher observation. The Standards for Literacy in History/Social Studies, Science and Technical Subjects are designed to inform literacy instruction across the disciplines and are also best matched to assessments anchored in those disciplines.

The College Board made a big show of its inclusion of topics from History and Science on all parts of the redesigned test. In fact, students now get special cross-test scores that show their performance on questions in these topics on all three subjects (including, oddly, Math). However, in practice, the content has not changed much from the old test. The SAT has always had Reading passages in History and in Science.

Reading for Literacy in History/Social Studies

The Reading section contains two passages in history/social studies and even gives a cross-test subscore using these questions. The passages include nonhistorical social studies topics like economics, as well as primary sources of historical importance. With the addition of primary source passages, this content area likely aligns better to the redesigned test. Most of these standards align in the same way the standards for Reading Informational Text do. One of the passages will contain a data representation and one may be a double passage.

Reading for Literacy in Science and Technical Subjects

The Reading section contains two passages in Science and even gives a cross-test subscore using these questions. The passages are drawn from a wide variety of scientific topics, both contemporary and historical. Most of these standards align in the same way the standards for Reading Informational Text do. One of the passages will contain a data representation and one may be a double passage.

Writing for Literacy in History/Social Studies, Science and Technical Subjects

The SAT Essay does not align well with these standards because the prompt is too narrow to support detailed historical and scientific content. The essay must be written specifically about the persuasive strategies of a given passage. That passage may contain historical or scientific content, but the student's essay must discuss the author's argument and rhetorical strategies, not the passage's topic itself.

Speaking and Listening

There is no speaking or listening component on either test. However, these activities are a normal part of classroom activities when preparing for essays. Furthermore, teachers can create and assign collaborative activities centered on almost any element of the test.

3

Reading Assignments

Probably the most crucial element of preparation for the Reading section of the SAT is *practice*. The point of the Reading section is to test whether students can understand a text, and students who are not strong readers cannot improve without spending time actually *reading*. But there's no reason you have to limit yourself to SAT material—there are things to read all around us. Even a passage as short as a single paragraph has a main idea, explicit statements, and implicit conclusions. You can take almost any passage at all, have students read it, and ask them questions about what they've read.

This document will help guide you through this process. We will give you tips on how to find an appropriate passage and how to write questions for it that reflect the kinds of questions that SAT Reading questions ask. The nice thing about the test is that there's little variation in the format and question types. Once you become familiar with it, it's easy to adapt existing texts into SAT style passages.

While this document specifically discusses SAT preparation, drills like this can be used for other purposes too. You can use these drills for ACT preparation as well, since ACT Reading questions are mostly identical to SAT questions. Or you can use them as pure reading comprehension drills for your regular English classes. The goal here is simply to get students to read effectively and efficiently.

Choosing a Passage

Here are some tips for choosing a text to use for your reading drill.

1. Passages Should Be Around 600 Words
SAT passages are around 500–750 words or 4–5 paragraphs, so that's a good length to aim for. Most newspaper articles tend to run slightly longer than that, but still well within reason. You should avoid anything over 1,000 words. Not only is it more difficult to keep students' attention that long, but longer articles will often present more complicated arguments or situations and provide more information than is necessary for our purposes. Of course, if you see a long article on a topic you like, you can always just use a smaller portion of it.

But remember too this is your class, not the real SAT. The degree to which you adhere to the 500–750 word limit is determined by the degree to which you want your drill to mimic a real SAT passage. If you want to make your assignment just a short quiz, great: use a one-paragraph passage with two questions. If you want it to be a larger project, you can pick something like a long-form article. Just know that the further you stray from 750 words, the less your passage will resemble the real SAT.

2. Use Online Newspapers
Online newspapers are perhaps the best and easiest source of freely available passages. They have articles on a variety of topics, usually written in clear but sophisticated language. Opinion pieces and editorials can be good sources because they're short and they have points of view and arguments, as opposed to more objective journalistic articles. But regular informative articles can also be effective.

We often use *The New York Times* website, since it is one of the most popular and respected sites, and it has a good breadth of topics. But any newspaper, national or local, will do fine. Magazines like *The Atlantic* or Internet-only news sites like *Slate* or *The Daily Beast* can also provide good content. Popular science sites like *Discover Magazine* are good places to find science articles that don't require too much preexisting knowledge.

You can even use sources that are less highbrow. Websites about sports, fashion, television, or even personal blogs can be used for these passages. In fact, using alternative material like this can show students that we read the same way no matter what we're reading. (If you do use nonnewspaper Internet sources, you will want to be sure to read the articles carefully first. The Internet can get a little vulgar at times.)

Please note that some websites may require a paid subscription for full access to articles. Before asking students to read online articles on their own, make sure they'll all have free access to the content.

And, of course, you needn't use the Internet; print newspapers and magazines work just as well, if you don't mind the extra photocopying.

Fiction passages also show up on the SAT, but it can sometimes be harder to create fiction passages yourself. Any piece of fiction will have to be excerpted—even short stories are generally too long for the test. You'd have to make sure that the excerpt you choose can stand alone without knowledge of the rest of the story, and that it doesn't require too much esoteric interpretation to understand. A passage can have a one- or two-sentence introductory paragraph that sets the basic scene, but too much background will distract from our goal.

You can use books you're reading in your class anyway, of course. If you're talking about *The Great Gatsby*, why not write some SAT-style questions about it? Just be careful to keep your questions limited to a specific passage without asking too much about larger themes that require understanding of the book as a whole. Remember that this is a test of reading comprehension, not a literature test.

3. Don't Require Outside Knowledge

Don't pick articles on topics that require too much outside knowledge. SAT passages are tests of how well students read, not how much they know. You don't want to penalize students who don't know much about the stock market, neurology, or international politics.

This doesn't mean you have to avoid complicated topics altogether. Science articles, for example, are often great sources of texts, because they're usually good about giving all the necessary background information in the articles themselves (and they often come with figures). The articles will address deep concepts, but you won't have to know anything ahead of time. This is why national newspapers are good sources for passages; they are written for a general audience and often don't assume much knowledge on the part of the reader. Conversely, more-specialized sites will often assume that the reader knows more about the subject. Articles about baseball statistics, for example, will be over the heads of any students who don't know anything about baseball.

4. Avoid Contentious Topics

Students may have strong opinions about certain political or religious topics like immigration, war, or abortion. Don't use articles that will start arguments among your students (or between you and your students). The point of these assignments is not to come to a resolution on a topic or to Find the Truth; it's just to understand *what the author says*. All that matters is what the article says, *not* whether it's true.

(Of course, if your class is actually working on a debate or on writing persuasive essays, you may want to discuss your students' own beliefs more. Do so at your own risk. But if you're only working on SAT prep, the students' own opinions on the topic are irrelevant to this assignment.)

5. Find Data

Remember that two passages out of five will have some sort of tables, graphs, or data representation, along with questions about those figures. If you want to work on data questions, you'll have to find an article that has figures.

Thankfully, there's no shortage of such things on the Internet. Some websites are dedicated to combining journalism with data analysis, like fivethirtyeight.com. Even mainstream sites like *The New York Times* or *Wall Street Journal* often use charts and graphs. They're out there, if you know to look for them.

6. Try a Double Passage

Every SAT has one double passage, in which students are given two different passages on similar or overlapping topics. You can easily make your own double passages by finding two articles on the same topic or event. If you do so, make sure the articles are sufficiently different from each other. Don't pick two straight journalistic articles from two different papers, since they'll most likely be very similar in tone and content. Instead, pick two articles of different types, such as an objective reportage article and an opinion piece on the same event.

7. Beware of Line Numbering

If you're working on SAT preparation, you will want your questions to have specific references to which part of the passage they're asking about. SAT passages come with line numbers, and almost all questions will give specific line numbers to let students know where in the passage they can find the answer. Obviously, most newspaper articles will not come with line numbers, so you will have to come up with a way to include these references.

If you're actually printing copies of the article, you can always write in line numbers by hand directly onto the paper. You don't have to number every line; SAT passages number every fifth line. Just make sure the line numbers you give in your questions properly match up to the passage.

If students are working on computers directly off the Internet, be careful. Different browsers can use different font sizes or column widths, so line numbers may differ, too. A word that appears in line 10 on your screen may appear in line 14 on a student's screen. In this case, rather than using line numbers when giving references, you can count sentences and paragraphs, e.g., "in the second sentence of paragraph two".

Writing the Questions

After you choose an article, you need to come up with some questions about it. Real SAT Reading questions are all multiple choice, but you can leave your questions open-ended. Writing effective answer choices is actually trickier and more time-consuming than it may seem. But the same skills and concepts are involved with open-ended questions, such as understanding main ideas, or going back to the passage to find evidence.

Students' answers to open-ended questions may vary wildly. As a result, some teachers might prefer to use these questions for group discussions instead of individual drills or homework, but that's up to you. If you are grading their responses, give students a little leeway if their responses aren't exactly what you expected, as long as they don't give too much, too little, or incorrect information.

Below we discuss nine main question types of SAT Reading passage questions, along with instructions for how to write your own. Sometimes we will provide a general question that can be asked about literally any passage. Other times we give a general template to be adapted to your passage or advice on how to craft specific questions about specific content. After this discussion, we'll present a passage along with some sample questions.

How many questions should you write for each passage? As many as you like! A five- or six-question drill about one question per type is a pretty manageable length. You can also choose to focus on one particular question type if you want to practice a particular skill. But there's no limit to the number of questions you could potentially ask about a text, depending on the length of the passage, its content, and your own interest in the topic. The SAT asks 10–11 questions about a single passage, so anything longer than that will likely be too much for your students.

1. Explicit Questions

These are questions that ask about things the author explicitly states in the passage. They're fairly easy to write. The key is to make the questions very literal: *What does the passage say about [X]?* Ask about facts and stated opinions explicitly presented in the passage.

Here are some hypothetical examples to give you a sense of what these questions sound like:

◆ **In the second sentence of paragraph 3, "decreasing test scores" are given as an example of what?**

- **According to the passage, how are "the larger monkeys" (line 24) different from "standard monkeys" (line 18)?**
- **In paragraph 4, the author states that "this proposed law" will have what consequence?**

Note that all these questions give specific references to what part of the passage you're asking about, be it a line number or a description of the sentence and paragraph. The SAT often gives specific line references, and learning to go back and check the passage is an important skill. Keep in mind that you don't have to point to the exact place where the answer is found; the answers to SAT questions are often found a sentence or two before or after the given line reference. (Unless of course you also want to ask an *evidence question*. More about those below.)

Remember that we only care about what the passage *says*, not whether it's *true* in real life. Some of your students may have other ideas about what the consequences of "this proposed law" will be. That doesn't matter. We are just trying to understand what the passage says.

It's perfectly fine to have your students directly quote the passage in order to answer the question. This helps reinforce the idea that the answers to the questions are all grounded in direct evidence from the passage. However, you may also want to practice *translation*. On the SAT, the correct answer choice will rarely use the exact same phrasing as the relevant line in the passage. Instead, the choice will have the same *meaning*, but use different words. It can be tough for some students to realize that a choice means the same thing as the line in the passage when it's worded differently. You may want to force your students to put their answers in their own words rather than quoting the passage to work on this skill. Doing so can also ensure that your students actually do understand the meaning of the passage, and they're not just blindly parroting the line.

2. Evidence Questions

One of the changes made to the SAT in 2016 was the introduction of Evidence questions. These are questions that specifically ask students to find evidence in the passage for their answer to an earlier question. These questions almost always take this form:

- **Which choice provides the best evidence for the answer to the previous question?**

The question then gives four possible line references in the choices. The previous question may be a question of any type—explicit, inferential, strategy, etc. We mentioned earlier that SAT questions usually contain line references so students know which part of the passage the question asks about. However, sometimes a question won't give a reference *because* the next question will ask a student to find it.

These questions work nicely with our strategies for the Reading section, since we already advocate finding textual justification for all your answers. They can often be done together with the previous question: if you can't find the line reference for the first question, check all the choices in the evidence question and see which one answers the first question.

Writing your own evidence questions is easy: just take any other question you've written, remove the line reference, and ask students to find the sentence that gives evidence for their answer. You could make these open-ended, forcing students to go find the evidence themselves. However, you may consider providing four possible choices in order to mimic the real test. That way, students can practice the technique of doing both questions in conjunction, testing the line references provided to see which answers the question. Keep in mind that choices on these questions on the SAT usually consist of one full sentence, so limit your choices accordingly.

3. Vocabulary-in-Context Questions

Vocabulary-in-Context questions test two things: vocabulary and context. They always take the same form:

> ◆ **In line [X], the word "[Y]" most closely means what?**

It will be up to you to choose a word to ask about. When choosing, consider both the word itself and the context around it.

Newspaper articles can often use vocabulary that is unfamiliar to students, so you can include questions as a straight vocabulary test: *do you know what this word means?* In fact, if you are giving a regular vocabulary assignment to your students, you can look for words from that assignment that appear in the passage.

While questions like that can be helpful for vocabulary building, Vocabulary-in-Context questions on the SAT are usually a little trickier than that. They don't just test hard or unfamiliar words; in fact, often the word *isn't* unfamiliar. Rather, it will be a familiar word that has multiple meanings, and students must use the context of the sentence in which it appears to determine which meaning is intended. For example:

◆ **In line [X], the word "fast" most closely means what?**

Everyone knows "fast" means "at a high speed". It's so obvious, it's hard for kids to define it without using the word ("It's when you go, uh, fast. You know, fast."). But that's not the only definition of "fast". It can also mean "firm" or "tight", as in *fast friends* or *the rope was tied fast to the pier*. Or it can mean "deeply", as in *fast asleep*. Or it can be a verb meaning "to abstain from eating for a period of time". Students may know all of these meanings, but they will have to look at the context to determine which meaning is intended in this particular sentence in the passage.

You can also pick words whose meanings are hard but can be deduced based on the content of the sentences in which they appear. But you should avoid using words that are overly specialized for the topic of passage. Scientific words fall into this category, but all fields use specialized words, including politics, business, and even sports. Be careful not to ask questions that demand too much outside knowledge. Our goal now is to help them learn to read effectively, not to teach them about mortgage insurance or electoral procedures.

On the real test, often these questions will have choices that are similar in meaning but have important nuanced differences. So, you don't want to be too lenient in allowing vague student answers. It can be hard for students to define a word without being given choices, so some lengthy or periphrastic answers are fine, as long as they're as specific as can be. Go further than just "good" or "bad".

4. Main Idea Questions

This is one of the most important question types and also one of the easiest to write. For every passage you use, you should ask:

◆ **What is the main idea of this passage?**

The answer to this question should *not* be a paragraph-long essay discussing the details of the author's argument. It should be a quick, one-sentence response briefly summarizing the article. All we're asking here is *what is it about?* For an informative piece, it's a quick description of the events or content. For an editorial, it's a quick summary of the position the author takes. For fiction, it's a summary of the action. It is not about nuance. You're basically asking to write a headline for the article.

You can also ask this question for individual paragraphs:

◆ **What is the main idea of the first paragraph?**
◆ **What is the main idea of the second paragraph?**

Et cetera. For these questions, students should focus on the *content* and *argument* of the paragraph in question, not necessarily mentioning its relationship to the article as a whole.

5. Strategy Questions

Strategy questions ask about how the article is constructed and why the author made the choices that he or she did. These can be on a larger level about the structure of the article, or on a small level asking about specific rhetorical techniques.

On the larger structural level, you can ask about the relationship between paragraphs. For example:

◆ **What is the relationship between the first paragraph and the passage as a whole?**

For a straightforward piece of reportage, the first paragraph will often give a brief summary of the events or situations that the article will go on to describe (i.e., the main idea of the passage). Opinion articles may use the first paragraph to state the argument they will give. But some passages might use the first paragraph to give necessary background information, to provide an anecdote that will illustrate a larger point later, to present a point of view it will then argue against, or even tell a story that is only tangentially related to the overall point.

Of course, you don't have to ask about the first paragraph. You can ask about any paragraph in the essay that has an interesting or unexpected relationship to the passage as a whole. The last paragraph also often has an interesting relationship to the passage as a whole.

On the smaller rhetorical level, you can look at specific choices that the author makes in the article you chose. The key is to ask *why* the author does something, or what the *function* of a particular line is. Some hypothetical examples and some potential responses follow:

- **In paragraph X, why does the author quote this person?**
  - to give evidence for his or her position
  - to provide a counterargument to a previous point
  - to lighten the tone of the passage
- **The question in line Y serves what function?**
  - to ask a rhetorical question for which the answer is obvious
  - to present the issue that will subsequently be debated
  - to present a mystery whose answer is still unknown

Notice that the example responses to the example questions do not have to make specific reference to the *content* of the article; rather they describe the *structure* and *form* of the article.

6. Inferential Questions

Writing inferential questions can be tricky. An inferential question asks students to find information that is unstated but necessarily implied by the passage. There are two important words in that description: *unstated* and *necessarily*.

First, make sure the answer isn't literally stated in the passage. Inferential questions on the SAT often ask what the passage "suggests" or "implies" in a given line. But it's not enough to just use the word "suggest" in your question. You need to make sure that the answer isn't stated outright. (And that it isn't stated in different words elsewhere in the passage.)

Second, make sure that the implication you seek is *necessarily* implied by the passage. This is not an exercise in conjecture or prediction. It is very important that you prevent your students from jumping to conclusions about the author's beliefs. Many wrong answer choices on the SAT rely on exactly that kind of guesswork.

When writing inferential questions, you should go easy on your students. Making inferences is an abstract reasoning skill. It's one of the hardest things that students will have to do on the test. But these questions are a bit easier on the SAT because students have four answer choices to scrutinize. They can pick up on clues given in the choices and eliminate those that are clearly false. Moreover, there may be multiple inferences that can be drawn from the line, and it may not be immediately obvious which one the question is asking for. If your questions don't have answer choices, you want to be sure to phrase them in such a way that helps students figure out specifically which inference you're looking for.

7. Tone Questions

This is a relatively rare question type, but it's another one that's easy to write. For any passage you use, you can ask:

◆ **What is the author's tone throughout the passage?**

Tone often comes down to positive/neutral/negative. The author argues for something, argues against something, or objectively reports facts. But, of course, you can get more subtle and varied in your description of the author's tone.

For example, the author could be

- ◆ Angry
- ◆ Enthusiastic
- ◆ Sarcastic
- ◆ Alarmed
- ◆ Nostalgic

As you make more drills, try to pick articles with varied tones. Don't use 10 articles that all have objective journalistic tone. Tones will more likely be varied in opinion and editorial pieces.

Remember also that the *tone* of a piece is not the same thing as the *content* of the piece. The author can be making a heavily biased argument on one side of an issue, yet still maintain an objective journalistic tone in his or her prose.

8. Data Questions

One of the changes in the redesigned test is the addition of data representations to passages, on both the Reading and the Writing tests. Questions will ask students to read and understand the figure, or to synthesize the information in the figure with what's written in the passage.

Obviously, in order to ask these questions, you'll need to find a passage that has a figure attached to it. But that isn't difficult at all! You can start with sites that specialize in data, fivethirtyeight.com most notable among them. But even regular newspaper articles are often supplemented by tables and graphs. Specialized scientific sites like *Discover* are also often fruitful sources. Sports sites are often fertile ground for data, but such data can often be very specialized, and you don't want to alienate students who may not follow the sport in question.

Questions can vary from simple to complex. On the simplest level, you can just ask students direct questions about the figure:

- **According to the figure, what were the company's profits in 2013?**
- **What was the lowest average temperature among the years shown in the graph?**

You can also directly connect the figure to the passage. You can make it an evidence question:

- **Where in the passage does the author make use of the information in the figure?**

You can make it a strategy question:

- **How does the author use the information in the figure to support his or her argument?**

You can even ask questions that can be answered using either the passage or the figure. For example, this question:

- **According to the passage and figure, what is the relationship between oceanic acidity and coral growth?**

. . . implies that the author explicitly discusses this relationship, but that the relationship also can be gleaned from the figure alone. Perhaps acidity and coral growth constitute the axes of a coordinate plane, and the shape of the line graph tells us the relationship.

9. Double Passage Questions

As we mentioned earlier, the SAT will contain a double passage. Double passages will present two passages on similar or overlapping topics. Many questions about double passages will be no different than regular questions, asking about particular details from one passage or the other. But some questions will ask students to identify or describe the relationship between the passages.

Finding two articles on the same topic is fairly easy to do. You could find two editorials that take opposite sides of an issue. You could find one objective report and one editorial. You could find two objective reports that are on different topics that have overlapping themes.

Double passage questions directly compare the form, content, or tone of the two passages. These can be questions of any type (explicit, inferential, strategy, etc.) as long as they address both passages. For example:

- **How would the author of Passage 1 most likely explain the "controversial results" mentioned in line 56 of Passage 2?**
- **How would the author of Passage 2 most likely respond to the argument presented in paragraph 2 of Passage 1?**
- **What person mentioned in Passage 2 holds views that are most similar to those of the author of Passage 1?**
- **In comparison with Passage 2, the tone of Passage 1 is more what?**
- **What rhetorical technique does Passage 1 employ that Passage 2 does not?**

Notice that these questions often ask for hypothetical responses: how *would* the author of Passage 1 respond to Passage 2? But these questions are always grounded in the explicit statements made in the passage. Be careful not to read too much into it and delve into conjecture. For example, just because an author makes an argument from a conservative point of view on one issue does not necessarily mean he or she would agree with Republican platforms on other issues. Only rely on what's stated in the passages, not your own beliefs or outside knowledge.

Giving the Assignment

You can make these passages a regular assignment throughout the year; say once a week or every other week. Find a passage, write some questions, and give it to your students. Since all Reading passages take basically the same format, you don't have to worry too much about varying your format. You'll want to pick a range of different source passages, of course, both from your own class readings or outside sources.

You might not include all question types on every assessment, but make sure they are all covered over the course of the semester. It's okay if one particular quiz doesn't have a strategy question, but you'll want to get one in there at some point. To help you determine the priority of question types, the following table shows the approximate distribution of question types on the practice tests the College Board has published so far:

Evidence Questions	18%
Vocab-in-Context Questions	17%
Explicit Questions	15%
Data Questions	10%
Main Idea Questions	10%
Inferential Questions	10%
Double Passage Questions	8%
Strategy Questions	8%
Tone Questions	4%

Additional Assignments

Here are some ideas for other ways you can adapt this assignment:

1. Demand Evidence for Every Question

As we can see in the chart above, evidence questions are the most common question type, so we know that finding textual support is an important skill. Rather than making separate questions for requesting evidence, you can make it a requirement for *every* question. No matter the question type, don't give line references. Force the students to provide a specific sentence, or even a single word, that justifies their answer.

2. Write Distractor Choices

As we've mentioned, one of the difficulties in multiple-choice tests like the SAT is the presence of distractor choices. These choices often aren't random—they're *tempting*. There are specific reasons why a student might believe that they're right.

It takes a long time to write choices for a question, so we wouldn't advise writing your own choices for all the questions. However, it's useful to provide students with at least one answer choice *that you explicitly tell them is wrong*. You can then ask the students, *why is this choice wrong?* What *specifically* makes it wrong? Give *specific textual evidence* proving that it's wrong.

This is exactly how the students should be approaching answer choices on the real test. There are three times as many wrong choices as there are right choices, so it's often easier to look for a wrong choice than it is to find the right choice. They should be going through the choices like a lawyer shooting down arguments, crossing out individual words that disqualify the entire choice.

3. Have Students Make the Drills

We've just talked about how easy it is to find passages and write questions—so why not have the kids do it themselves? Besides being less work for all of us (whoo!), getting them to see the principles behind the construction of the test can help them better understand what the test is asking them to do.

This can be a fun group project as well, with each member of a team doing a different step:

- Have Student A find a passage, either from texts you're already using in class or through their own research. If you like, you can let them have fun with this and choose less serious texts to use as passages.
- Have Student B write questions about the passage. Make sure they're already familiar with the different question types before asking them to do this.
- Have Student C take the assignment and write full explanations for why the answers are correct.
- Have Student D write distractor choices and explain why they're wrong.

Or, make an assembly line where each student does each step and then passes it to the right for the next step. At the end, you'll have four drills, each of which was built by all four students. You can then even have that group swap drills with a different group and try each other's drills.

98 ◆ Reading Assignments

Sample Passage

The following passage was taken from the opening paragraphs of *Jude the Obscure*, by Thomas Hardy, 1895.

[1] The schoolmaster was leaving the village, and everybody seemed sorry. The miller at Cresscombe lent him the small white tilted cart and horse to carry his goods to the city of his destination, about twenty miles off, such a vehicle proving of quite sufficient size for the departing teacher's effects. For the schoolhouse had been partly furnished by the managers, and the only cumbersome article possessed by the master, in addition to the packing-case of books, was a cottage piano that he had bought at an auction during the year in which he thought of learning instrumental music. But the enthusiasm having waned he had never acquired any skill in playing, and the purchased article had been a perpetual trouble to him ever since in moving house.

[2] The rector had gone away for the day, being a man who disliked the sight of changes. He did not mean to return till the evening, when the new school-teacher would have arrived and settled in, and everything would be smooth again.

[3] The blacksmith, the farm bailiff, and the schoolmaster himself were standing in perplexed attitudes in the parlour before the instrument. The master had remarked that even if he got it into the cart he should not know what to do with it on his arrival at Christminster, the city he was bound for, since he was only going into temporary lodgings just at first.

[4] A little boy of eleven, who had been thoughtfully assisting in the packing, joined the group of men, and as they rubbed their chins he spoke up, blushing at the sound of his own voice: "Aunt has got a great fuel-house, and it could be put there, perhaps, till you've found a place to settle in, sir."

[5] "A proper good notion," said the blacksmith.

[6] It was decided that a deputation should wait on the boy's aunt—an old maiden resident—and ask her if she would house the piano till Mr. Phillotson should send for it. The smith and the bailiff started to see about the practicability of the suggested shelter, and the boy and the schoolmaster were left standing alone.

[7] "Sorry I am going, Jude?" asked the latter kindly.

[8] Tears rose into the boy's eyes, for he was not among the regular day scholars, who came unromantically close to the schoolmaster's life, but one who had attended the night school only during the present teacher's

term of office. The regular scholars, if the truth must be told, stood at the present moment afar off, like certain historic disciples, indisposed to any enthusiastic volunteering of aid.

[9] The boy awkwardly opened the book he held in his hand, which Mr. Phillotson had bestowed on him as a parting gift, and admitted that he was sorry.

[10] "So am I," said Mr. Phillotson.

[11] "Why do you go, sir?" asked the boy.

[12] "Ah—that would be a long story. You wouldn't understand my reasons, Jude. You will, perhaps, when you are older."

[13] "I think I should now, sir."

[14] "Well—don't speak of this everywhere. You know what a university is, and a university degree? It is the necessary hallmark of a man who wants to do anything in teaching. My scheme, or dream, is to be a university graduate, and then to be ordained. By going to live at Christminster, or near it, I shall be at headquarters, so to speak, and if my scheme is practicable at all, I consider that being on the spot will afford me a better chance of carrying it out than I should have elsewhere."

[15] The smith and his companion returned. Old Miss Fawley's fuel-house was dry, and eminently practicable; and she seemed willing to give the instrument standing-room there. It was accordingly left in the school till the evening, when more hands would be available for removing it; and the schoolmaster gave a final glance round.

[16] The boy Jude assisted in loading some small articles, and at nine o'clock Mr. Phillotson mounted beside his box of books and other *impedimenta*, and bade his friends good-bye.

[17] "I shan't forget you, Jude," he said, smiling, as the cart moved off. "Be a good boy, remember; and be kind to animals and birds, and read all you can. And if ever you come to Christminster remember you hunt me out for old acquaintance' sake."

Sample Questions

Main Idea Question

1. What happens in the passage?

Vocabulary-in-Context Questions

2. In context, what does "effects" mean (paragraph 1, sentence 2)?
3. In context, what does "afford" mean (paragraph 14, sentence 5)?

Explicit Questions

4. According to the passage, why does Mr. Phillotson not take his piano with him?
5. According to the passage, why is Mr. Phillotson moving away?
6. How is Jude's reaction to Mr. Phillotson's departure different from that of the other students?

Evidence Questions

7. Which paragraph and sentence provides evidence for your answer to question 4?
8. Which paragraph and sentence provides evidence for your answer to question 5?

Inferential Question

9. Paragraph 2 suggests what about how the rector feels about Mr. Phillotson's departure?

Tone Question

10. Jude responds to Mr. Phillotson's departure with what emotion?

Answers and Explanations

The Passage

This passage is not a perfect example of a reading passage—not much happens here, it rambles at the end—so it's unlikely it would appear in this form on a real SAT. But we're not looking for a perfect reading passage. We're not actually writing an SAT; we're showing that you can apply SAT skills to *any* passage. This passage is certainly satisfactory for our purposes: it's 717 words (right in our target range of 500–750); it's the opening of the book, so it's fairly self-contained and doesn't require expository background; it has some difficult language, but not so much as to make the entire piece incomprehensible. It's a good start for us.

Don't worry about explaining too much. You don't have to tell kids anything about the book, what it's about, what happens later, the historical context, and so forth. You might want to (it's really good!) but you don't have to. Just focus on what's written. You might also be tempted to explain or define tough words like *"impedimenta"* in paragraph 16, but, again, you don't have to. You're better off forcing them to deal with the fact that they'll sometimes see words they don't know.

The Questions

Let's look at some possible answers to these questions. We don't have choices, so your answers may vary. Note that for the sake of clarity the questions here are phrased slightly differently than they would be if they had answer choices. On the real test, questions are usually phrased as incomplete sentences that can be completed with the correct answer. Question 10, for example, would be written as "Jude responds to Mr. Phillotson's departure with . . ."

Main Idea Question

1. *What happens in the passage?*

   For fiction passages, instead of asking for the main idea or purpose of the passage, questions will often simply ask what happens in the passage. Remember that we are not looking for a paragraph answer here. We want a *one-line summary*, enough to fit in an answer choice.

   How about: **a boy says goodbye as a schoolteacher moves away**. That's all we need. Notice that we didn't even refer to

102 ◆ Reading Assignments

the characters' names, a common occurrence for questions of this type.

Vocabulary-in-Context Questions

2. *In context, what does "effects" mean (paragraph 1, sentence 2)?*

   For these questions, we must go back to the original sentence:

   > *The miller at Cresscombe lent him the small white tilted cart and horse to carry his goods to the city of his destination, about twenty miles off, such a vehicle proving of quite sufficient size for the departing teacher's* **effects**.

   Imagine the word in question wasn't there, just a blank, and we had to fill in that blank with another word. What word would we pick? Something like **belongings** would work.

3. *In context, what does "afford" mean (paragraph 14, sentence 5)?*

   Once again, let's go back to the sentence.

   > *By going to live at Christminster, or near it, I shall be at headquarters, so to speak, and if my scheme is practicable at all, I consider that being on the spot will* **afford** *me a better chance of carrying it out than I should have elsewhere.*

   What fits in that blank? Perhaps **provide**.

Explicit Questions

4. *According to the passage, why does Mr. Phillotson not take his piano with him?*

   The answer to this is not tricky, but it may be tricky to know where to look. In this case, there are two reasons he's not taking the piano. First, paragraph 1 says he only has a small cart, so **it won't fit**. Second, paragraph 3 tells us that "even if he got it into the cart he should not know what to do with it on his arrival at Christminster, the city he was bound for, since he was only going into temporary lodgings just at first." So, **he has nowhere to put it**.

Reading Assignments ◆ 103

5. *According to the passage, why is Mr. Phillotson moving away?*

   Again, the hardest part is simply finding the answer (though
   here it might be a bit easier because we already read the
   most important lines in question 3 above). Try paragraph
   14. There, Mr. Phillotson says he wants "to be a university
   graduate" and living in Christminster will make that easier.
   In short, **he's going to college.**

6. *How is Jude's reaction to Mr. Phillotson's departure different from
   that of the other students?*

   The other students are mentioned in paragraph 8. While Jude
   is helping Mr. Phillotson pack his things, the other boys **do not
   help** and stand off to the side. The key here is to be sure not to
   read too much into the passage. We must stick to what it says.
   We don't know for sure why they do this (although we may have
   guesses). All we know for sure is what they do (or don't do).

Evidence Questions

7. *Which paragraph and sentence provides evidence for your answer
   to question 4?*

   Evidence questions are best done in conjunction with the
   questions they describe, so you can do this at the same time
   as question 4. (We grouped the questions by type here, but
   on the real SAT, a question like this would come immediately
   after question 4, thus it's easier to do them together.) As we
   already saw, the best evidence is in **paragraph 3, sentence 2.**

8. *Which paragraph and sentence provides evidence for your answer
   to question 5?*

   Once again, this is best done concurrently with question 5. As
   we saw, the best evidence is in **paragraph 14, sentence 5.**

Inferential Question

9. *Paragraph 2 suggests what about how the rector feels about
   Mr. Phillotson's departure?*

   Now we have a question where we can't simply look up the
   answer. We have to deduce it based on what is written. Let's
   look at paragraph 2:

104 ◆ Reading Assignments

All paragraph 2 says about the rector's feelings is that he does not like change, and that he therefore does not want to see the teacher leave. So he **considers the teacher's departure to be a significant change**. *Not* that he doesn't like the teacher, *not* that he's afraid, *not* that he likes the new teacher better. Any of those may well be true, but none are implied by the sentences in paragraph 2. Learning to make inferences also means learning not to infer *too much*.

Tone Question

10. *Jude responds to Mr. Phillotson's departure with what emotion?*

For fiction passages, tone questions often focus on the characters' emotional states rather than the tone of the narration itself (which is usually neutral). Here, we can see it right in paragraph 8: there are *tears* in his eyes. He is **sad** that his teacher is leaving. The real test will likely have more difficult choices than just "sadness", but starting this simple is a great first step toward getting to the right answer.

4

Writing Assignments

The Reading test, the Writing test, and the Essay are all separate sections, each with its own set of skills, but they overlap in interesting ways. Students' Reading and Writing are combined in the EBRAW score, while the Essay score is kept separate. But actually, the Essay shares more with each of those tests than they share with each other. To wit:

◆ The Essay prompt requires you to read and analyze a given passage. The skills needed to do so are roughly the same skills needed for the passages on the Reading test.
◆ The Essay also requires you to (surprise!) write an essay. Doing so requires understanding of rules of grammar, usage, and rhetoric, which are explicitly tested on the Writing test.

It may be tempting to spend less time on the Essay in your preparation because it's optional and many colleges will not require it, and that's understandable. However, *the act of preparing* for the essay helps strengthen skills that students will need on Reading and Writing. While the essay itself may not be as important, working on the essay can have multiplicative effects beyond the essay itself.

In this chapter, we will begin by briefly discussing the format of the Essay. Then we will give several options for how to work the SAT Essay into your classes, either as direct preparation for the SAT, or as a source for longer-term projects.

106 ◆ Writing Assignments

Format

We discussed this in Part I, but here's a refresher. Every essay prompt will begin with this introduction before the passage:

As you read the passage below, consider how [the author] uses

- ◆ evidence, such as facts or examples, to support claims.
- ◆ reasoning to develop ideas and to connect claims and evidence.
- ◆ stylistic or persuasive elements, such as word choice or appeals to emotion, to add power to the ideas expressed.

This is followed by a persuasive passage around 600–750 words long. Every prompt will have a version of this text after the passage:

Write an essay in which you explain how [the author] builds an argument to persuade [his or her] audience that [the author's claim]. In your essay, analyze how [the author] uses one or more of the features listed in the box above (or features of your own choice) to strengthen the logic and persuasiveness of [his or her] argument. Be sure that your analysis focuses on the most relevant features of the passage. Your essay should not explain whether you agree with [the author's] claims, but rather explain how [the author] builds an argument to persuade [his or her] audience.

Students will receive scores from 2 to 8 in three different categories:

- ◆ **Reading**: How well does the student understand the content of the passage?
- ◆ **Analysis**: How well does the student analyze the author's rhetorical strategies and their effect?
- ◆ **Writing**: How well is the essay written?

The 2–8 scale is composed of two scores of 1–4, each given by a different reader. When we talk about scores here, we'll be using the 1–4 scale because that's the scale that the readers use. Readers do not look at an essay and think, "that's a 5". There's no such thing as a 5. A 5 means that one reader thought "that's a 2" and another thought "that's a 3".

Which Scores Are Most Important?

They're equally important. It's possible that in the future colleges will place more weight on one aspect of the score over the others, but right now this scoring system is still new. We have no idea how colleges are going to value these scores (if they do at all), so we'll treat them all equally.

We also don't know what counts as a "good" score. If the scores range from 2 to 8, then the median is 5, so we would expect that to be the average. (If you multiply them by 100, they'll look just like "regular" SAT scores—200 to 800 with 500 in the middle.) But, of course, the median doesn't have to be the mean, and mean scores will probably vary among the three categories. We'll know more once we have more real test data available.

For your purposes, a "good" score is one that is higher than where your students begin. A 2–2–2 is a good score if a student started with a 1–1–1, but not if they started with a 3–3–3. Like *all* SAT scores, because students might start from a wide range of scoring levels, it's best to think of them in terms of *improvement*, not in terms of absolute benchmarks.

As such, you should adjust your preparation based on the needs of your students. If they struggle with writing, you should focus on that first. It doesn't matter how well they understood the passage if they can't communicate what they've read. Analysis is harder than Reading, so it's best to focus on the latter first before addressing the former.

108 ◆ Writing Assignments

Practice Tests

If your school is offering full-length practice tests, you should consider including the essay. You can get official essay prompts directly from the College Board in the same place that the practice tests are given.

Scheduling fully proctored tests can be very difficult; few schools have a spare 3 hours and 50 minutes lying around. Schools often offer the PSAT to sophomores and juniors, which is great, but the PSAT has no essay so that doesn't help us here.

If you want to give a proctored test but you're having trouble scheduling the time, you should consider skipping the essay. However, you can still give the essay separately at a different time. It's likely easier to find 50 minutes of free time.

It's certainly an option to assign essays as homework, but then you can't enforce the time limit. Timing on the redesigned essay is a lot more generous than timing on the old essay was (only 25 minutes!), but timing still can be problem for some students. All practice tests produce more accurate scores (i.e., predictive of real test scores) when given under real test conditions. As such, it's best to give the essay as part of the full test; writing an essay in isolation is a different experience than writing one after having just sat through 3 hours of multiple-choice sections (the last hour of which was math). But timed sections in isolation are still better than untimed sections. If you can't find 50 straight minutes, don't break it up over multiple sessions; assign it for homework and have them time themselves. It's better for them to do it in one session, like on the real test, even if it is at home.

Additional Prompts

Like full tests, there are only a handful of official SAT practice prompts available. As of this writing, there are five: four with the four practice tests, plus another one in the "sample problems" (the sample problems contain two prompts, but one is repeated on the practice tests). By summer 2016, there will likely be a sixth after the College Board releases one of the real spring tests. Six is more than enough to go with full practice tests (you're probably not going to give more than six proctored tests), but if you want proctored tests *and* in-class practice, you may want more.

We've already discussed some ways to find texts to use as reading passages. The same texts can potentially be used for essay prompts. The source passage will be 600–750 words—about the same length as a reading passage, slightly longer. The only requirement for the content of the passage is that it should be some form of *persuasive* essay. The prompt asks students to evaluate the author's strategies in building an argument, so there needs to be an argument to be evaluated.

That limits your potential sources to an extent. Fiction in general is unsuitable (though not out of the question; you might find an exhortative passage within a work of fiction). Newspaper articles won't work when they're straight reportage, but op-eds would do nicely. Certainly there's no shortage of historical political speeches that would be excellent candidates. And the Internet has no shortage of fierce polemics. Just remember again that students should not need any factual knowledge of the issue in order to write the essay. All necessary information should be provided for them. If you'd like to use an outside source that requires a bit of background explanation, you should provide it ahead of time. (The SAT generally doesn't provide background for essay passages, but the passages are usually self-explanatory. Reading passages do sometimes have a brief introductory paragraph giving background or context.)

How to Score the Essay

A-List offers an essay scoring service for schools that use our online test assessment portal. If you want to give the essay as part of a full practice test, or if you simply have a lot of essays to grade, contact A-List to help you.

The alternative is to grade the essays yourself. The College Board provides a scoring rubric for the essay on their website and in the *Official SAT Study Guide*. Additionally, while they do not provide sample essays for the four prompts that come with practice tests, there are samples for the two prompts in the "sample question" set. Reviewing these essays can be very enlightening, particularly when compared with each other. Looking at the difference between a 4–1–3 and a 4–3–4, for example, is the best way to understand what the Analysis score means, by showing you an essay that did everything well except analysis.

Ideally, student essays should be read by two people, each giving scores in the three categories. However, it may be difficult for you to enlist your colleagues to assist you. If you're the only one reading it, simply give the students one set of scores on the 4-point scale. Don't give scores on the 2–8 scale. When people attempt that, they tend to start to make too fine a distinction: "Hmm, is this a 5 or a 6? It's kind of a 5-and-a-half ..." Don't do that. An essay can't be "a 5". It can only be "a 2" and "a 3". If a student gets a 5, that just means two people disagree about whether it's a 2 or a 3.

Reading and Analysis

Students should still find main ideas for each paragraph and the main idea for the passage (though the latter is given to you in the text after the passage). Students should communicate through their essay that they've understood the content of the passage—that's what the "Reading" score evaluates.

Remember, though, that the essay requires you to read a little bit differently than the Reading test does. The essay is not a book report. Besides the content of the argument, students must also discuss the *form* of the argument. What rhetorical strategies were used? What sort of logical reasoning was provided? What evidence? What stylistic flourishes? And beyond simply listing the tactics in the passage, the students should discuss *why* those tactics are used. What is the effect of starting with a personal anecdote in the first paragraph? How does that transition to the scientific data in the second paragraph? That's not to say that such questions don't appear on the Reading test—they certainly do, in Strategy questions for example—but such questions are in the minority of reading questions, whereas it's the crux of the topic on the essay.

Wait, That Sounds Hard

It is hard! Analysis is much harder for students than Reading is. As we mentioned earlier, you should adjust your classroom according to your class's needs. If you've got ELL students or others who struggle to read and write English, don't worry about Analysis *at all*. If you can get them scoring 3–1–3, or even just 2–1–2, you've done a good job. On the other hand, if you have students who are already competent-to-good readers, you should push them to go beyond simply reading the passage into analysis.

Revision

You can work on improving Reading and Analysis scores through group discussions without students writing a single word on the page. But the only way to improve Writing scores is by writing. But simply writing over and over again won't make your writing any better. Students need to examine their essays to see how to improve them.

You no doubt already do a fair share of writing work in your classes, so you don't need us to tell you how to discuss essays. But let's take some time to discuss how to treat the quirks of SAT essays.

In-Test Revision

During the test, students do have some opportunity for revision. The old SAT essay was too short (only 25 minutes! that's insane!) for students to do even a cursory reread of their essays. With 50 minutes, students have a bit more of a cushion such that they may be able to review their essays. They can't do major rewrites, but they can look it over, correct some careless spelling or grammatical errors, strike redundancies or add in a clarifying statement or two. (The readers know that this is a handwritten essay in a time limit, so it's totally fine to have ugly cross-outs or carets sticking words in the middle of sentences.)

After the test, you'll want to review the students' essays with them. This could be done privately by writing comments on their essays (test graders will not provide comments, only scores). It's often helpful to discuss essays publicly with the whole class, in order to demonstrate common problems that occur frequently. (If you do discuss student work publicly, you'll want to give students anonymity so they don't feel ashamed about their weaknesses.) Having students work in small groups to workshop each other's essays can also be great, but you want to be sure they know what to look for. If every student in a group got a 1 on Writing, there's no guarantee that teaming up will make their work any better.

If you'd prefer not to use real student essays, you can use the sample student essays the College Board provided in the practice problems. Those are particularly nice because they provide a range of different scores. You can see a 1–1–1 and a 4–4–4 and everything in between. The downside is that there aren't sample student essays available for every prompt. If the sample essays are for a prompt they haven't done, then they'll have to read the passage before you review the samples.

The Writing and Language Test

When reviewing and discussing these essays, you should do so in the framework of *the same categories tested on the Writing test.* These categories are:

- ◆ **Expression of Ideas**
  - *Development*: How your argument unfolds; adding or deleting sentences
  - *Organization*: Sequencing of sentences and paragraphs; transitions
  - *Effective Language Use*: Word choice; tone; redundancy; conciseness; vagueness
- ◆ **Standard English Conventions**
  - *Usage*: Grammar and relationships between words: verbs; pronouns; idioms
  - *Sentence Structure*: Relationships between clauses; run-ons; fragments; modifiers
  - *Punctuation*: Commas; colons; semicolons; periods

The Writing Test is passage-based in order to mimic the act of editing an essay. So when you're *actually* editing an essay, you should be thinking about making the same kinds of changes you've seen on multiple-choice writing questions.

Do this *explicitly*. If you prepare a student essay to discuss in front of the class, take note of the kinds of problems you found in it. Then go find SAT Writing questions that test the same errors, such as subject-verb agreement, redundant expressions, vague language, improper transition words, and many more. This way, you can prepare for the essay and the Writing test at the same time. It reinforces the idea that the things you're asked on the multiple-choice questions aren't arbitrary annoyances—they're the things you do to make your writing better. The act of reviewing the essay strengthens the rules you discussed for the Writing test.

It's important to note that all six of these categories are important. Teachers often get pulled too much in only one direction. Some spend all their time talking about content and development. That's great—that affects your Reading and Analysis scores too. But it's meaningless if your language is unidiomatic to the point of nonfluency. Others spend all their time circling commas and pronouns and spelling errors. That's great—sloppy writing obscures your argument. But you also want to make sure the argument makes sense.

A New Draft

It's fun to review and discuss essays (well, maybe not fun, but useful), but why not go further and *have students actually rewrite their essays*. Make it a homework assignment so they can take their time with it. Have them take their notes from the classroom discussion and apply it to their own work to make it better.

These edits should not be drastic. Students shouldn't entirely rewrite the essay from scratch. Don't add five more paragraphs. (But do feel free to split your one-long-paragraph essay into five coherent paragraphs.) You can place limits on what they do to ensure it's a revision, e.g., page limits or requiring a certain amount of the original essay remains unchanged. Don't write a new essay; just make what you already have better. They don't even necessarily have to take into account their Reading and Analysis scores here. It could be purely a revision based on the language and rhetoric of their own arguments, depending on which skills you want to focus on.

Obviously, this task is outside of the scope of the SAT. Once those 50 minutes are up, the essays are done. If a student got a 1 Writing score timed and revised it into a 3 Writing score, that doesn't mean they'll be able to get a 3 on the first try during a timed section. But the fact that they can push it up to a 3 means it's *possible*. Some kids literally have no idea what good writing looks like. Getting them to recognize the difference between good and bad writing is valuable in its own right. And it can be a big confidence boost for them to know that they are capable of producing good writing.

Expand the Assignment

As we saw in Part II, several of the Common Core Standards do not align with the SAT Essay because the standards require more extensive writing than a single 50-minute essay allows. However, if these standards are important to your class, you can stretch SAT Essay prompts to longer and more ambitious assignments.

Research to Build and Present Knowledge

Writing standards 7, 8, and 9 focus on research, obviously outside the scope of the 50-minute SAT Essay. But the essay prompts are great jumping-off points for research projects.

The source passages for the prompts come from a range of topics, both historical and scientific. These are the sources for the four prompts on the College Board's website:

Test	Author	Source	Thesis
1	Jimmy Carter	Foreword to *Arctic National Wildlife Refuge: Seasons of Life and Land, a Photographic Journey*, Subhankar Banerjee, 2003.	The Arctic National Wildlife Refuge should not be developed for industry.
2	Martin Luther King, Jr.	"Beyond Vietnam—A Time to Break Silence." Speech delivered in New York City on April 4, 1967.	American involvement in the Vietnam War is unjust.
3	Eliana Dockterman	"The Digital Parent Trap," *Time*, August 19, 2013.	There are benefits to exposure to technology in early childhood.
4	Paul Bogard	"Let There Be Dark," *Los Angeles Times*, December 21, 2012.	Natural darkness should be preserved.

As you can see, these are all topics that can be fertile ground for additional discussion beyond the 700-word passage provided.

First of all, have students look for additional sources that address the same issue. For historical sources, there can be a plethora of options—students should not have difficulty finding sources about activism against the Vietnam War. For more contemporary topics, like the value of screen time for young children, it may require a bit more digging.

Additional sources can be of a variety of types. Some may be more objective reporting to give the historical context of the topic: what is the situation, how has it arisen, why is anyone talking about this. But it's also important to find more *opinions* on the issue. Remember that each passage is a persuasive essay. The author has a clear and definite perspective. Try to find a different source that argues *a contrasting perspective*. This can show you possible responses to the main passage, or the ideas that the main passage was responding to.

Remember also that our task on the SAT Essay is not to evaluate the truth of the author's perspective but to analyze how he or she makes the argument. You can do the same for the additional sources you find. Does the second source use similar tactics or different tactics? Better yet, find another source that argues the *same* position as the original passage, but using *different tactics*. Compare their effectiveness: which passage makes a better case?

Production and Distribution of Writing

Writing Standards 4, 5, and 6 are about the production and distribution of writing. Standards 4 and 5 we've already discussed: the former is about the production of writing and the latter about revision. Standard 6 is about the use of technology in writing. Again, that's outside the scope of the 50-minute SAT Essay, but easily within the scope of an extended research project.

First of all, if the students are doing research at all, chances are they'll be using the Internet. Hopefully, they'll go beyond Googling the topic and clicking on the first link that mentions it. If they don't, that's something you can work on with them: how to do more extensive and effective research. You don't have to roam the basement halls of a library's periodical room, but you do have to go beyond Wikipedia.

Secondly, they can use technology in their actual writing. The standard mentions using the Internet for publishing and collaboration, which is something you can definitely have your students do. Instead of individual projects, assign these research tasks to teams. Have them set up webpages to discuss their findings and come up with new perspectives. Log these conversations so you can see how their theses develop.

Third, they can incorporate multimedia elements into their final presentations. Does one of the passages cite any data or statistics? Find the source of those figures. Make a table or graph showing those numbers. Or make representations of other numbers you find in your research. As we've seen on both the Reading and Writing tests, the redesigned test is a big fan of incorporating data representations into passages. Students should have seen enough of these by now that they can take a crack at making their own figures.

Range of Writing

Standard 10 emphasized writing "routinely over extended time frames (time for research, reflection, and revision) and shorter time frames (a single sitting or a day or two) for a range of tasks, purposes, and audiences". That's certainly applicable to the kind of research project we describe here. We start with a short-term project like the actual SAT Essay prompt. We adapt that essay with reflection and revision through several drafts. Then we expand the task into a larger research project or presentation that could stretch over several weeks. You could even stretch the assignment over the entire semester, if you like. The topic is pliable enough to be slipped into whatever time frame you have available.

Essay Assignment Summary

I. Basic Practice and Revision

1. Find a passage to assign. It could be a real SAT prompt or any persuasive essay 600–750 words long.
2. Have students write a 1–4 page essay about the passage according to the standard SAT prompt.
    a. Ideally this will be as part of a full-practice test.
    b. If not, try to administer it separately in a timed 50-minute session.
    c. If that's not possible, assign it for homework.
3. Grade the essays, either by yourself, with a colleague, or using A-List.
4. Discuss essays with the students. There are several ways you could do this:
    a. Give individual comments on students' essays.
    b. Discuss anonymized student essays with the entire class.
    c. Discuss the College Board's sample student essays with the entire class.
    d. Have students workshop each other's essays together in small groups.
5. When discussing essays, do so in the context of the Writing test categories:
    a. Development
    b. Organization
    c. Effective Language Use
    d. Usage
    e. Sentence Structure
    f. Punctuation
6. Have students use notes to revise their essays.
7. Regrade the essays and give feedback about what's improved.

II. Extended Research

1. Choose an SAT prompt to your liking. It can be one they've already written about, but it doesn't have to be.
2. Have students research additional sources on the same topic discussed in the prompt's passage and build a writing assignment around it.
    a. Look for historical background and write about the context of the issue.

118 ◆ Writing Assignments

      b. Find sources that argue the same point as the prompt.

      c. Find sources that argue a contrasting point from the prompt.

      d. Write about how the different sources use similar or different rhetorical and argumentative tactics.

      e. Write about how the different tactics shape the effectiveness of their arguments.

3. Use technology in research and writing production.

      a. Use the Internet for research (effectively!).

      b. Use the Internet to collaborate with other students and log conversations.

      c. Use multimedia sources to supplement the project with tables, graphs, and other figures.

4. Extend this project over whatever time period you have available, from a multipage paper to a longer in-class presentation.

Appendix
All ELA Alignment Tables

How to Read the Tables

Each anchor standard is shown in a table followed by the grade-specific standard for grades 11–12. Each table contains columns showing:

- The code for the standard, as defined by the CCSSI
- The standard itself
- Its alignment with the SAT

Each standard has a code containing three parts: letters denoting the strand or content area, the grade level of the standard or "CCR" for anchor standards, and the sequential number of the standard (sometimes with letters for subpoints). For example, "RL.CCR.5" refers to the fifth anchor standard in the Reading Literature strand, and "W.11-12.3a" refers to the first subskill of the third standard for the grade 11–12 standard in the Writing strand.

The two alignment columns will each display one of the following symbols:

- **Y** = The standard is aligned with the test in question.
- **N** = The standard is not aligned with the test in question.
- **P** = The standard is partially aligned with the test in question. This means a qualifying comment was listed for the standard in the original alignment document.

Reading CCR Anchor Standards

Code	Standard	Aligns
Key Ideas and Details		
R.CCR.1	Read closely to determine what the text says explicitly and to make logical inferences from it; cite specific textual evidence when writing or speaking to support conclusions drawn from the text.	**P**
R.CCR.2	Determine central ideas or themes of a text and analyze their development; summarize the key supporting details and ideas.	**Y**
R.CCR.3	Analyze how and why individuals, events, and ideas develop and interact over the course of a text.	**Y**
Craft and Structure		
R.CCR.4	Interpret words and phrases as they are used in a text, including determining technical, connotative, and figurative meanings, and analyze how specific word choices shape meaning or tone.	**Y**
R.CCR.5	Analyze the structure of texts, including how specific sentences, paragraphs, and larger portions of the text (e.g., a section, chapter, scene, or stanza) relate to each other and the whole.	**Y**
R.CCR.6	Assess how point of view or purpose shapes the content and style of a text.	**Y**
Integration of Knowledge and Ideas		
R.CCR.7	Integrate and evaluate content presented in diverse formats and media, including visually and quantitatively, as well as in words.	**Y**
R.CCR.8	Delineate and evaluate the argument and specific claims in a text, including the validity of the reasoning as well as the relevance and sufficiency of the evidence.	**Y**
R.CCR.9	Analyze how two or more texts address similar themes or topics in order to build knowledge or to compare the approaches the authors take.	**P**
Range of Reading and Level of Text Complexity		
R.CCR.10	Read and comprehend complex literary and informational texts independently and proficiently.	**Y**

Appendix: All ELA Alignment Tables ◆ 121

Reading Standards for Literature

Code	Standard	Aligns
Key Ideas and Details		
RL.11-12.1	Cite strong and thorough textual evidence to support analysis of what the text says explicitly as well as inferences drawn from the text, including determining where the text leaves matters uncertain.	**P**
RL.11-12.2	Determine two or more themes or central ideas of a text and analyze their development over the course of the text, including how they interact and build on one another to produce a complex account; provide an objective summary of the text.	**Y**
RL.11-12.3	Analyze the impact of the author's choices regarding how to develop and relate elements of a story or drama (e.g., where a story is set, how the action is ordered, how the characters are introduced and developed).	**Y**
Craft and Structure		
RL.11-12.4	Determine the meaning of words and phrases as they are used in the text, including figurative and connotative meanings; analyze the impact of specific word choices on meaning and tone, including words with multiple meanings or language that is particularly fresh, engaging, or beautiful. (Include Shakespeare as well as other authors.)	**Y**
RL.11-12.5	Analyze how an author's choices concerning how to structure specific parts of a text (e.g., the choice of where to begin or end a story, the choice to provide a comedic or tragic resolution) contribute to its overall structure and meaning as well as its aesthetic impact.	**Y**
RL.11-12.6	Analyze a case in which grasping point of view requires distinguishing what is directly stated in a text from what is really meant (e.g., satire, sarcasm, irony, or understatement).	**Y**
Integration of Knowledge and Ideas		
RL.11-12.7	Analyze multiple interpretations of a story, drama, or poem (e.g., recorded or live production of a play or recorded novel or poetry), evaluating how each version interprets the source text. (Include at least one play by Shakespeare and one play by an American dramatist.)	**N**

(Continued)

Code	Standard	Aligns
RL.11-12.8	(Not applicable to literature)	—
RL.11-12.9	Demonstrate knowledge of eighteenth-, nineteenth-, and early-twentieth-century foundational works of American literature, including how two or more texts from the same period treat similar themes or topics.	**N**

Range of Reading and Level of Text Complexity

Code	Standard	Aligns
RL.11-12.10	By the end of grade 11, read and comprehend literature, including stories, dramas, and poems, in the grades 11–CCR text complexity band proficiently, with scaffolding as needed at the high end of the range. By the end of grade 12, read and comprehend literature, including stories, dramas, and poems, at the high end of the grades 11–CCR text complexity band independently and proficiently.	**Y**

Reading Standards for Informational Text

Code	Standard	Aligns
Key Ideas and Details		
RI.11-12.1	Cite strong and thorough textual evidence to support analysis of what the text says explicitly as well as inferences drawn from the text, including determining where the text leaves matters uncertain.	**P**
RI.11-12.2	Determine two or more central ideas of a text and analyze their development over the course of the text, including how they interact and build on one another to provide a complex analysis; provide an objective summary of the text.	**Y**
RI.11-12.3	Analyze a complex set of ideas or sequence of events and explain how specific individuals, ideas, or events interact and develop over the course of the text.	**Y**
Craft and Structure		
RI.11-12.4	Determine the meaning of words and phrases as they are used in a text, including figurative, connotative, and technical meanings; analyze how an author uses and refines the meaning of a key term or terms over the course of a text (e.g., how Madison defines faction in Federalist No. 10).	**Y**
RI.11-12.5	Analyze and evaluate the effectiveness of the structure an author uses in his or her exposition or argument, including whether the structure makes points clear, convincing, and engaging.	**Y**
RI.11-12.6	Determine an author's point of view or purpose in a text in which the rhetoric is particularly effective, analyzing how style and content contribute to the power, persuasiveness, or beauty of the text.	**Y**
Integration of Knowledge and Ideas		
RI.11-12.7	Integrate and evaluate multiple sources of information presented in different media or formats (e.g., visually, quantitatively) as well as in words in order to address a question or solve a problem.	**Y**
RI.11-12.8	Delineate and evaluate the reasoning in seminal U.S. texts, including the application of constitutional principles and use of legal reasoning (e.g., in U.S. Supreme Court majority opinions and dissents) and the premises, purposes, and arguments in works of public advocacy (e.g., The Federalist, presidential addresses).	**Y**

(Continued)

Code	Standard	Aligns
RI.11-12.9	Analyze seventeenth-, eighteenth-, and nineteenth-century foundational U.S. documents of historical and literary significance (including The Declaration of Independence, the Preamble to the Constitution, the Bill of Rights, and Lincoln's Second Inaugural Address) for their themes, purposes, and rhetorical features.	Y

Range of Reading and Level of Text Complexity

Code	Standard	Aligns
RI.11-12.10	By the end of grade 11, read and comprehend literary nonfiction in the grades 11–CCR text complexity band proficiently, with scaffolding as needed at the high end of the range. By the end of grade 12, read and comprehend literary nonfiction at the high end of the grades 11–CCR text complexity band independently and proficiently.	Y

Writing CCR Anchor Standards

Code	Standard	Aligns
Text Types and Purposes		
W.CCR.1	Write arguments to support claims in an analysis of substantive topics or texts, using valid reasoning and relevant and sufficient evidence.	**YE**
W.CCR.2	Write informative/explanatory texts to examine and convey complex ideas and information clearly and accurately through the effective selection, organization, and analysis of content.	**YE**
W.CCR.3	Write narratives to develop real or imagined experiences or events using effective technique, well-chosen details, and well-structured event sequences.	**N**
Production and Distribution of Writing		
W.CCR.4	Produce clear and coherent writing in which the development, organization, and style are appropriate to task, purpose, and audience.	**YE**
W.CCR.5	Develop and strengthen writing as needed by planning, revising, editing, rewriting, or trying a new approach.	**PWE**
W.CCR.6	Use technology, including the Internet, to produce and publish writing and to interact and collaborate with others.	**N**
Research to Build and Present Knowledge		
W.CCR.7	Conduct short as well as more sustained research projects based on focused questions, demonstrating understanding of the subject under investigation.	**N**
W.CCR.8	Gather relevant information from multiple print and digital sources, assess the credibility and accuracy of each source, and integrate the information while avoiding plagiarism.	**N**
W.CCR.9	Draw evidence from literary or informational texts to support analysis, reflection, and research.	**PE**
Range of Writing		
W.CCR.10	Write routinely over extended time frames (time for research, reflection, and revision) and shorter time frames (a single sitting or a day or two) for a range of tasks, purposes, and audiences.	**P/N**

Writing Grades 11–12 Standards

Code	Standard	Aligns
Text Types and Purposes		
W.11-12.1a	Introduce precise, knowledgeable claim(s), establish the significance of the claim(s), distinguish the claim(s) from alternate or opposing claim(s), counterclaims, reasons, and evidence.	**YE**
W.11-12.1b	Develop claim(s) and counterclaims fairly and thoroughly, supplying the most relevant evidence for each while pointing out the strengths and limitations of both in a manner that anticipates the audience's knowledge level, concerns, values, and possible biases.	**YE**
W.11-12.1c	Use words, phrases, and clauses as well as varied syntax to link the major sections of the text, create cohesion, and clarify the relationships between claim(s) and reasons, between reasons and evidence, and between claim(s) and counterclaims.	**YWE**
W.11-12.1d	Establish and maintain a formal style and objective tone while attending to the norms and conventions of the discipline in which they are writing.	**YE**
W.11-12.1e	Provide a concluding statement or section that follows from and supports the argument presented.	**YW**
W.11-12.2a	Introduce a topic; organize complex ideas, concepts, and information so that each new element builds on that which preceded it to create a unified whole; include formatting (e.g., headings), graphics (e.g., figures, tables), and multimedia when useful to aiding comprehension.	**YE**
W.11-12.2b	Develop the topic thoroughly by selecting the most significant and relevant facts, extended definitions, concrete details, quotations, or other information and examples appropriate to the audience's knowledge of the topic.	**YE**
W.11-12.2c	Use appropriate and varied transitions and syntax to link the major sections of the text, create cohesion, and clarify the relationships among complex ideas and concepts.	**YWE**
W.11-12.2d	Use precise language, domain-specific vocabulary, and techniques such as metaphor, simile, and analogy to manage the complexity of the topic.	**YE**
W.11-12.2e	Establish and maintain a formal style and objective tone while attending to the norms and conventions of the discipline in which they are writing.	**YE**

Appendix: All ELA Alignment Tables ◆ 127

Code	Standard	Aligns
W.11-12.2f	Provide a concluding statement or section that follows from and supports the argument presented (e.g., articulating implications or the significance of the topic).	**YW**
W.11-12.3a	Engage and orient the reader by setting out a problem, situation, or observation and its significance, establishing one or multiple point(s) of view, and introducing a narrator and/or characters; create a smooth progression of experiences or events.	**N**
W.11-12.3b	Use narrative techniques, such as dialogue, pacing, description, reflection, and multiple plot lines, to develop experiences, events, and/or characters.	**N**
W.11-12.3c	Use a variety of techniques to sequence events so that they build on one another to create a coherent whole and build toward a particular tone and outcome (e.g., a sense of mystery, suspense, growth, or resolution).	**N**
W.11-12.3d	Use precise words and phrases, telling details, and sensory language to convey a vivid picture of the experiences, events, setting, and/or characters.	**YW**
W.11-12.3e	Provide a conclusion that follows from and reflects on what is experienced, observed, or resolved over the course of the narrative.	**YW**
Production and Distribution of Writing		
W.11-12.4	(Grade-specific expectations for writing types are defined in standards 1–3.)	—
W.11-12.5	Develop and strengthen writing as needed by planning, revising, editing, rewriting, or trying a new approach, focusing on addressing what is most significant for a specific purpose and audience. (Editing for conventions should demonstrate command of Language standards 1–3 up to and including grades 11–12.)	**PWE**
W.11-12.6	Use technology, including the Internet, to produce, publish, and update individual or share writing products in response to ongoing feedback, including new arguments or information.	**N**
Research to Build and Present Knowledge		
W.11-12.7	Conduct short as well as more sustained research projects to answer a question (including a self-generated question) or solve a problem, narrow or broaden the inquiry when appropriate; synthesize multiple sources on the subject, demonstrating understanding of the subject under investigation.	**N**

(Continued)

Code	Standard	Aligns
W.11-12.8	Gather relevant information from multiple authoritative print and digital sources, using advanced searches effectively; assess the strengths and limitations of each source in terms of the task, purpose, and audience; integrate the information into the text selectively to maintain the flow of ideas, avoiding plagiarism and overreliance on any one source and following a standard format for citation.	**N**
W.11-12.9a	Apply grades 11–12 Reading standards to literature (e.g., "Demonstrate knowledge of eighteenth-, nineteenth-, and early-twentieth-century foundational works of American literature, including how two or more texts from the same period treat similar themes or topics.").	**PE**
W.11-12.9b	Apply grades 11–12 Reading standards to literary nonfiction (e.g., "Delineate and evaluate the reasoning in seminal U.S. texts, including the application of constitutional principles and use of legal reasoning [e.g., in U.S. Supreme Court Case majority opinions and dissents] and the premises, purposes, and arguments in works of public advocacy [e.g., The Federalist, presidential addresses].").	**YE**
Range of Writing		
W.11-12.10	Write routinely over extended time frames (time for research, reflection, and revision) and shorter time frames (a single sitting or a day or two) for a range of tasks, purposes, and audiences.	**P/N**

Language CCR Anchor Standards

Code	Standard	Aligns
Conventions of Standard English		
L.CCR.1	Demonstrate command of the conventions of standard English grammar and usage when writing or speaking.	**YW**
L.CCR.2	Demonstrate command of the conventions of standard English capitalization, punctuation, and spelling when writing.	**YW**
Knowledge of Language		
L.CCR.3	Apply knowledge of language to understand how language functions in different contexts, to make effective choices for meaning or style, and to comprehend more fully when reading or listening.	**YW**
Vocabulary Acquisition and Use		
L.CCR.4	Determine or clarify the meaning of unknown and multiple-meaning words and phrases by using context clues, analyzing meaningful word parts, and consulting general and specialized reference materials, as appropriate.	**YR**
L.CCR.5	Demonstrate understanding of figurative language, word relationships, and nuances in word meanings.	**YR**
L.CCR.6	Acquire and use accurately a range of general academic and domain-specific words and phrases sufficient for reading, writing, speaking, and listening at the college and career readiness level; demonstrate independence in gathering vocabulary knowledge when considering a word or phrase important to comprehension or expression.	**PRW**

130 ◆ Appendix: All ELA Alignment Tables

Language Grades 11–12 Standards

Code	Standard	Aligns
Conventions of Standard English		
L.11-12.1a	Apply the understanding that usage is a matter of convention, can change over time, and is sometimes contested.	**N**
L.11-12.1b	Resolve issues of complex or contested usage, consulting references (e.g., *Merriam-Webster's Dictionary of English Usage*, *Garner's Modern American Usage*) as needed.	**N**
L.11-12.2a	Observe hyphenation conventions.	**YW**
L.11-12.2b	Spell correctly.	**YW**
Knowledge of Language		
L.11-12.3a	Vary syntax for effect, consulting references (e.g., Tufte's *Artful Sentences*) for guidance as needed; apply an understanding of syntax to the study of complex tasks when reading.	**YW**
Vocabulary Acquisition and Use		
L.11-12.4	Determine or clarify the meaning of unknown and multiple-meaning words and phrases based on grades 11–12 reading and content, choosing flexibly from a range of strategies.	—
L.11-12.4a	Use context (e.g., the overall meaning of a sentence, paragraph, or text; a word's position or function in a sentence) as a clue to the meaning of a word or phrase.	**YR**
L.11-12.4b	Identify and correctly use patterns of word changes that indicate different meanings or parts of speech (e.g., conceive, conception, conceivable).	**N**
L.11-12.4c	Consult general and specialized reference materials (e.g., dictionaries, glossaries, thesauruses), both print and digital, to find the pronunciation of a word or determine or clarify its precise meaning, its part of speech, its etymology, or its standard usage.	**N**
L.11-12.4d	Verify the preliminary determination of the meaning of a word or phrase (e.g., by checking the inferred meaning in context or in a dictionary).	**YR**
L.11-12.5a	Interpret figures of speech (e.g., hyperbole, paradox) in context and analyze their role in the text.	**YR**
L.11-12.5b	Analyze nuances in the meaning of words with similar denotations.	**YR**
L.11-12.6	Acquire and use accurately a range of general academic and domain-specific words and phrases sufficient for reading, writing, speaking, and listening at the college and career readiness level; demonstrate independence in gathering vocabulary knowledge when considering a word or phrase important to comprehension or expression.	**PRW**

Progressive Skills

Code	Skill	Aligns
L.3.1f	Ensure subject–verb and pronoun–antecedent agreement.	**Y**
L.3.3a	Choose words and phrases for effect.	**Y**
L.4.1f	Produce complete sentences, recognizing and correcting inappropriate fragments and run-ons.	**Y**
L.4.1g	Correctly use frequently confused words (e.g., to/too/two; there/their).	**Y**
L.4.3a	Choose words and phrases to convey ideas precisely. (Subsumed by L.7.3a.)	—
L.4.3b	Choose punctuation for effect.	**Y**
L.5.1d	Recognize and correct inappropriate shifts in verb tense.	**Y**
L.5.2a	Use punctuation to separate items in a series. (Subsumed by L.9-10.1a.)	**Y**
L.6.1c	Recognize and correct inappropriate shifts in pronoun number and person.	**Y**
L.6.1d	Recognize and correct vague pronouns (i.e., ones with unclear or ambiguous antecedents).	**Y**
L.6.1e	Recognize variations from standard English in their own and others' writing and speaking, and identify and use strategies to improve expression in conventional language.	**Y**
L.6.2a	Use punctuation (commas, parentheses, dashes) to set off nonrestrictive/parenthetical elements.	**Y**
L.6.3a	Vary sentence patterns for meaning, reader/listener interest, and style. (Subsumed by L.11-12.3a.)	**Y**
L.6.3b	Maintain consistency in style and tone.	**Y**
L.7.1c	Place phrases and clauses within a sentence, recognizing and correcting misplaced and dangling modifiers.	**Y**
L.7.3a	Choose language that expresses ideas precisely and concisely, recognizing and eliminating wordiness and redundancy.	**Y**
L.8.1d	Recognize and correct inappropriate shifts in verb voice and mood.	**Y**
L.9-10.1a	Use parallel structure.	**Y**

Additional Resources

A-List

Main website: www.alisteducation.com
Bookstore: www.alisteducation.com/bookstore

The SAT

Main website: http://sat.collegeboard.org/home
Test specifications for the redesigned SAT (pdf): https://
collegereadiness.collegeboard.org/pdf/test-specifications-
redesigned-sat-1.pdf
Free practice tests: https://collegereadiness.collegeboard.org/sat/
practice/full-length-practice-tests
The same practice tests are also available in *The Official SAT Study
Guide*, College Board, 2015.
Additional sample questions: https://collegereadiness.collegeboard.
org/sample-questions
Essay scoring rubric: https://collegereadiness.collegeboard.org/sat/
scores/understanding-scores/essay
College Board Guide to Implementing the Redesigned SAT (pdf):
https://collegereadiness.collegeboard.org/pdf/college-board-
guide-implementing-redesigned-sat-installment-2.pdf
CCSS Alignment (no longer on the College Board's website):
"Common Core State Standards Alignment: Readistep ™, PSAT/
NMSQT ™ and SAT ™," Natasha Vasavada, Elaine Carman, Beth
Hart, and Danielle Luisier, College Board, 2010.
Additional practice at Khan Academy (requires free login): www.
khanacademy.org/

The Common Core State Standards

Main website: www.corestandards.org/
The Standards (available to read on the web or as pdf downloads):
www.corestandards.org/the-standards

Taylor & Francis eBooks

Helping you to choose the right eBooks for your Library

Add Routledge titles to your library's digital collection today. Taylor and Francis ebooks contains over 50,000 titles in the Humanities, Social Sciences, Behavioural Sciences, Built Environment and Law.

Choose from a range of subject packages or create your own!

Benefits for you
- Free MARC records
- COUNTER-compliant usage statistics
- Flexible purchase and pricing options
- All titles DRM-free.

Benefits for your user
- Off-site, anytime access via Athens or referring URL
- Print or copy pages or chapters
- Full content search
- Bookmark, highlight and annotate text
- Access to thousands of pages of quality research at the click of a button.

REQUEST YOUR **FREE** INSTITUTIONAL TRIAL TODAY

Free Trials Available
We offer free trials to qualifying academic, corporate and government customers.

eCollections – Choose from over 30 subject eCollections, including:

Archaeology	Language Learning
Architecture	Law
Asian Studies	Literature
Business & Management	Media & Communication
Classical Studies	Middle East Studies
Construction	Music
Creative & Media Arts	Philosophy
Criminology & Criminal Justice	Planning
Economics	Politics
Education	Psychology & Mental Health
Energy	Religion
Engineering	Security
English Language & Linguistics	Social Work
Environment & Sustainability	Sociology
Geography	Sport
Health Studies	Theatre & Performance
History	Tourism, Hospitality & Events

For more information, pricing enquiries or to order a free trial, please contact your local sales team:
www.tandfebooks.com/page/sales

 Routledge
Taylor & Francis Group

The home of Routledge books

www.tandfebooks.com